# INSIDE ZHAN ZHUANG

## Mark Cohen



First Edition

ISBN 978-0-9883178-8-8

## Dedication

This book is for all those seeking to understand more.
And to the fearless who are willing to brave the journey
inside themselves in order to discover a source of knowledge
that never ceases.

# CONTENTS

# PREFACE

The body holds many secrets and if you 'listen,' it will tell you. At the time of this writing very little has been said about what *actually happens* during the Standing Meditation exercise. What really drives the process of transformation? What makes it possible and how does it work? It is these and other mysteries that we shall explore.

If the Chinese are anything they are practical, and many of their instructions in the form of poetic axioms have very specific meanings and applications, once one has the key. This can be an alchemical solution, a metaphor or an understanding innate to the Chinese culture of years gone by. In the past these elements have created some confusion which has led to misrepresentations, or in the worst cases outright errors. Add to that the deliberate omissions and 'red-herrings,' stemming from times when knowledge of certain truths meant the difference between life and death, and you begin to see some of the challenges one faces in their search to discover how Zhan Zhuang really works.

Finally, this book is not for the faint-hearted. Real achievement requires serious work and study. Therefore a basic knowledge of the body's physical and energetic structures becomes an integral part of the advanced curriculum, both for health and healing and the internal martial arts. I will say this much, the road of accomplishment is not an easy one, but the rewards are truly worth the effort, both now and for the future.

Mark Cohen
December 2012

# INTRODUCTION

The concept of this work is a little different than the typical manual or how-to book. Instead I've approached the presentation of material as if the reader were participating or observing a number of private lessons. Therefore, don't be surprised by interesting digressions from time to time where I point out various relevant elements that perhaps others may not have thought of or equated with the subject under discussion.

The material presented here is a product of many years of personal experience and my own individual journey on the road of achievement. Your experiences may be different. But there are certain commonalities encountered by nearly all at various stages of development.

One thing is sure; achievement requires both dedication as well as experimentation and trial-and-error. *Wang Xiang Zhai* exhorted his students to do just that. Part of this process is the ability to let go of preconceived notions and embrace the possibilities of the unknown. This letting go is one of the keys at every level of advancement.

All methods presented herein have been tested and verified on myself. However they do require enough proper attention and focus along with plenty of Kung Fu - perseverance, time and effort, in order to succeed.

In many of the photographic sequences I have included examples of both myself and Cynthia, a first year student to show that when one begins training, it is often necessary to modify the postures due to injury or other bodily limitations. This means essentially reducing the amount of stretch or dynamic tension to preserve a unified integrity. The idea here is to accept yourself exactly how you are at the present moment and go from there. This way, as the body opens up over time, the postures will naturally assemble and inflate of themselves, until they reach their optimum balance and efficiency.

# RESOURCES

In this day and age, the easiest way to access the additional resource material needed for an in depth understanding of this work, is to do so *online*. For acupuncture points and channel diagrams, you can bookmark Yin Yang House, *http://www.yinyanghouse.com/acupuncturepoints/locations_theory_and_clinical_applications* although there are also a number of others. For diagrams and locations of the various muscles, I recommend *Wikipedia*. Wikipedia's drawings come from the famous Gray's Anatomy Textbook.

# LIST OF CHANNEL ABBREVIATIONS

| | |
|---|---|
| LU | Lung |
| LI | Large Intestine |
| ST | Stomach |
| SP | Spleen |
| HT | Heart |
| SI | Small Intestine |
| BL | Bladder |
| K | Kidneys |
| P | Pericardium |
| TB | Triple Burner |
| GB | Gall Bladder |
| LIV | Liver |
| GV | Governing Vessel |
| CV | Conception Vessel |

# UNDERSTANDING THE BASICS

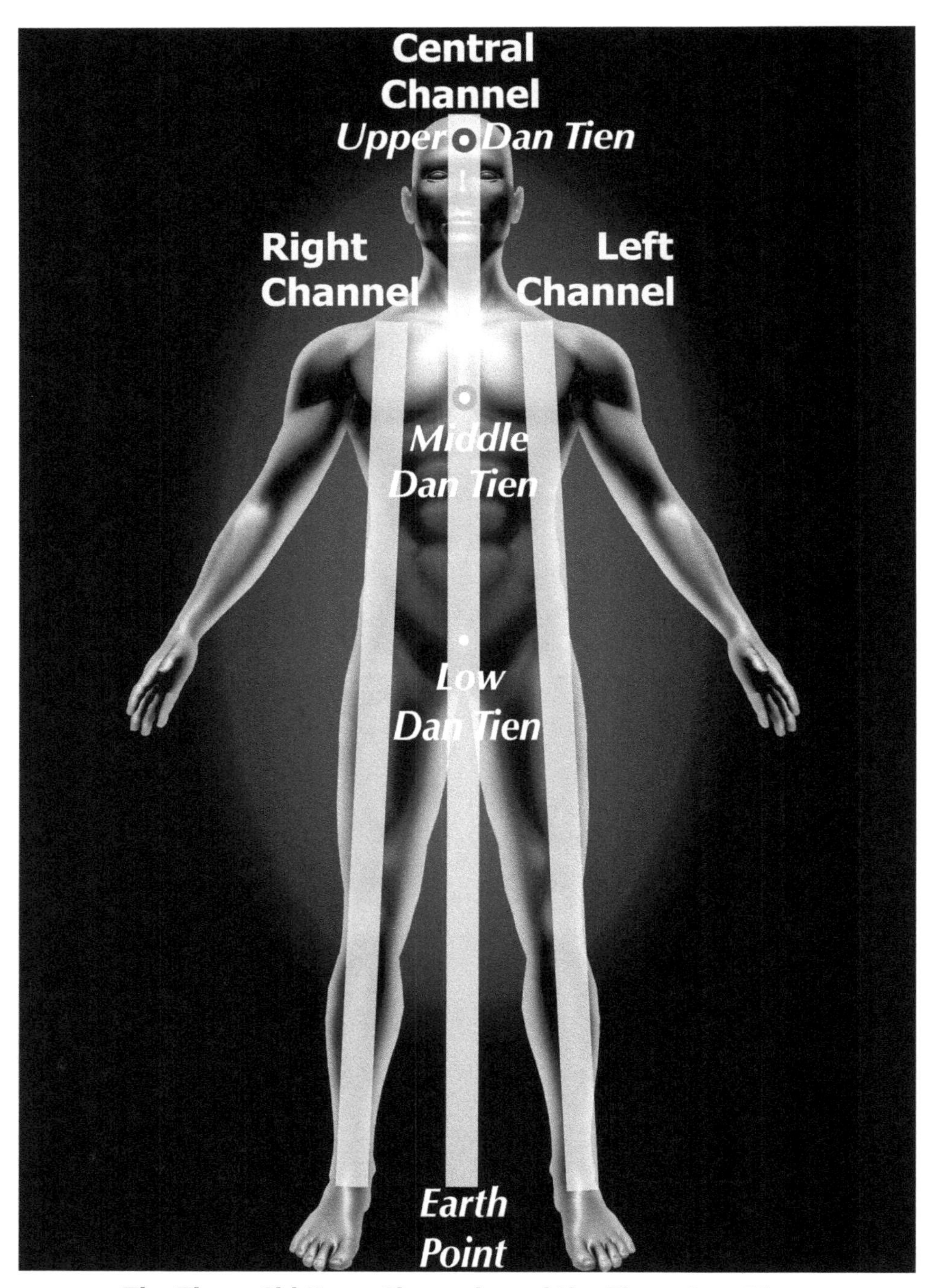


**The Three Chi Kung Channels and the Three Dan Tiens**

## THE THREE CHI KUNG CHANNELS

The human body has many energetic overlays, structures or matrixes embedded within it and around it. According to Taoist theory the three deep *Chi Kung* Channels were created first and are the progenitors of the Acupuncture Channels. All three major *Chi Kung* Channels begin above *Baihui* GV-20 and tangibly separate at the Upper Dan Tien.

The Central Channel descends through core of the body to *Huiyin* CV-1 at the Perineum and on down to the Earth Point. It also passes through the marrow of the bones of the upper and lower extremities and rejoins the etheric energy-body at the feet and hands. The Left and Right Channels descend through the center of both sides of the head, through the center of Shoulder's Nests, midriff and *Kua* on down to below the feet and out the hands. Whereas the Central Channel passed through center of the bones of the upper and lower extremities, the Left and Right Channels follow the outsides of the bones along the same route.

## THE THREE DAN TIENS

The three Dan Tiens are energetic locations within the body which are the seats of various transformations. These should not be confused with the *Sanjiao*, or Triple Burner of Chinese medicine. The confusion often stems from the fact the lower *Jiao* (burning space) is in the same location as the low Dan Tien and the upper *Jiao* is in the same region as the middle Dan Tien. Whereas the three Dan Tiens are regions of *Jing*, *Chi* and *Shen* transformations respectively, the three *Jiao* share responsibility for reproduction and elimination, (lower) digestion and absorption (middle) and circulation and respiration. (upper) For the purposes of this work we will primarily concern ourselves with the low Dan Tien.

## THE THREE CATEGORIES OF DEVELOPMENT

When one begins Zhan Zhuang training their goals generally fall into one of three categories: health and longevity, internal martial power and mental and spiritual development.

Since most all achievement in these three areas is based on greater and greater relaxation and integration, standing meditation naturally becomes an excellent method for rapid accomplishment.

So, we find a suitable location, get ourselves into position, correct our alignments, center our feeling-awareness in the low (or upper) Dan Tien and then what?

It is obvious that over time much happens to the individual during Zhan Zhuang practice, such as the transformation of the nerves, healing of various injuries, the acquisition of genuine internal power and even energizing the brain and expanding consciousness.

It is fair to say that nearly all great internal martial artists of the previous centuries acquired their achievement to a large extent by first passing through the gate of Zhan Zhuang. This includes Yang Cheng Fu who trained Zhan Zhuang but only taught it to a handful of people.

So the question becomes, how did the famous practitioners of old achieve such great accomplishments? What occurred inside their bodies that allowed them to reach such high levels?

The answer to this question has three components: Physical, Energetic, and the *Shen* force. Shen force can be thought of as a combination of *Xin* - heart/mind and *Yi* – intention, as well as that part of us which controls both.

Of these three energetic components, the physical aspect is the primary requisite for without the physical transformation, none of the three categories of development can be fulfilled.

It is very hard to develop martial power and nigh on impossible to expand consciousness through Zhan Zhuang without the health of the physical body. In terms of Chinese Medicine, this is seen as the free and unobstructed flow of Chi throughout the organism.

So the question becomes, can there be some development without the perfection of the above? Of course. Once one reaches a certain point in resolving blockages, glimpses of many of the higher and more efficient functional states become possible.

Naturally, the goal of our training is to be able to replicate these states at will, which, as anyone who's tried will confirm, is not so easy. The difficulty often lies in the practitioner's current state of consciousness.

So here we can see the clear inter-merging of the health and the mental development aspects. Of course a similar relationship also exists between health and healing and martial power. The body's health is essential in developing the proper structure and linkage necessary to generate the abundant Chi required to issue effective *Jing*.

It is important to recognize this interconnection of the three categories at the outset. The best scenario regarding long term practice might go something like this; Zhan Zhuang's healing ability steadily improves the body which one day leads to what the Taoists call 'radiant health.'

This abundant energy and strength is then directed into moving the Chi through all the channels for martial application. This has the added effect of further improving the body's health. And lastly all this may eventually lead to an the even more advanced state in which one lets go of power altogether to allow the higher energies to enter and imbue one's body, mind and spirit with deeper states of consciousness.

Now you can see why the health aspect is of such fundamental importance. Martial development requires both health *and* power practices. The mental aspect, the development of consciousness takes this a step further, utilizing the energy gained in *both* the healing and martial aspects, but in a different manner. This refers in part to the so-called alchemical techniques which lead to greater awareness.

The amazing thing about Zhan Zhuang is that if one practices diligently over the years, many of these alchemical transformations manifest of themselves. Like one of my teachers once put it when speaking of long term training, "...if you practice long enough, *things happen*." And he was right!

## HEALTH AND LONGEVITY

The practitioners of the past had a strong motivation to train, and to gain enough power to win out and survive life and death combat. But all that changed with the advent of firearms. Today the practitioners who have the strongest motivation are often those with some sort of health problem.

It is my experience that a proper course of standing meditation can help correct or heal many conditions, both external and internal. It does so by using the body's own 'innate wisdom' and with a good dose of common sense.

The exact methods used will vary with the specific problem or imbalance, but no matter how one starts, there are certain common principals of development. Basically Zhan Zhuang uses relaxation and a constantly refining balance to loosen the muscles and sinews and open Chi flow in order to correct imbalances.

In addition to deepening the body's overall relaxation, Zhan Zhuang also greatly increases body awareness, perception and other forms of awareness as well. This will be discussed in more detail later, but for now it is enough to know the general principal.

Zhan Zhuang for health is approached somewhat differently than when used to develop martial power and effectiveness. Firstly, our focus is far more internal, often with eyes closed. We also tend to emphasize the relaxation element over rigid postural integrity. (Chi flows best through relaxed muscles.)

This emphasis leads us to respect the postural limitations of our 'weakest link,' in other words, an injured or fragile area.

That said, there are circumstances like systemic deficient conditions, where we do practice with our eyes open in order to absorb external energy to augment the body's Chi. But for the most part, closing the eyes is preferred for health, because of its ability to adequately contain our Chi and keep it from escaping during practice.

In today's world, now more than ever, the practice of Zhan Zhuang, especially for health is the antithesis of the types of frenetic, stressful and chaotic energies one encounters in everyday life.

Science is now beginning to prove the effect of stress and hyperactivity in causing diseases. Repeated exposure to these energies generally breaks down a person's immune system, leaving them vulnerable. Zhan Zhuang's ability to repair and replenish these and other energies goes a long way in preventing problems before they start, as well as healing those already upon us.

In addition, there is the factor of stillness in standing meditation. This idea of a calm, placid stillness goes a long way in 'soothing the savage beast,' meaning that it pacifies the mind, emotions and nervous system. This in turn helps reverse and balance the over-amped sensory input all too familiar to most in their daily lives.

With this sense of peace instilled in the mind, body and emotions, one is better able to meet the challenges sure to arise if one continues their practices. I'm speaking here of the resolution of past and present karmic and life patterns which often play out during the course of long term daily training, especially as our perception and awareness increases. This not only refers to the balancing of past and present causes and effects in the body, but also in the emotions, mind and even spirit, involving such things as one's strong likes and dislikes, fears, phobias, intense desires and more.

## INTERNAL MARTIAL POWER

As far as internal martial arts are concerned, standing meditation is a most vital practice, that is, if one wants to obtain a really serious achievement. In most cases in the past it was a closely guarded secret.

All the great martial artists of years gone by were taught it, and why? Because dedicated practice unifies the body's Chi faster and more completely than any other method.

The three major internal styles all use a form of Zhan Zhuang to develop power. In *Xingyi* it's the *Santi* posture, in *Bagua* its the pidgin-toed stances and other standing postures and in *Tai Chi* it's the *Wuji* posture at the beginning of the form as well as a number of the various Tai Chi form postures.

The truth is, if one is diligent in their practice, even though they are still, it often happens that they feel the awakenings of many types of Jing energy.

Fa Jing ability can never reach a highly refined level without unifying the body and mind, in other words without meditation.

And standing meditation is a most efficient and formidable way to accomplish this. The intuitive knowledge of the body and its pathways coming from Zhan Zhuang makes moving the energy necessary for the many types of Fa Jing much easier.

Also, and equally as important, standing meditation allows one's Fa Jing to be expressed in the paraphrased words of *Wang Xiang Zhai*, "...small movement is better than large movement, no movement is better than small movement."

One of the best ways to develop this sort of ability is by using the series, 'Eight Postures for Martial Arts,' found later in this book. This was the first series I was shown.

It's eight postures develop the Chi and body structure such that eventually any point on the body can become a weapon. That is, Jing can be issued from anywhere in the body not just the hands, arms or feet.

Long ago it was my experience that after many years of Kung Fu and Tai Chi training, much of what was talked about in the 'Classics' was just that, talk. In other words, there was no way to bridge the gap between what I could do and what I read about as being possible.

But all that changed with Zhan Zhuang practice. After enough time standing, certain energies espoused in the Classics began to manifest in my body. And the interesting thing was that these quantum leaps in awareness were instantaneous. One moment I didn't know and the next I not only knew, but could also *do*.

This has continued over the years and with a little experimentation many of the techniques once shrouded in mystery have become clear in both mind and body.

By concentrating long enough on the low Dan Tien, the center of our physical power and health, eventually one experiences an awakening, or 'little enlightenment' of that center.

When this actually occurs for a person there are generally two manifestations that will confirm this. The first is physical and emotional feelings of invincible martial power. The second is a similar feeling regarding one's sexual energy.

Now these are the feelings, not necessarily the actual demonstrable abilities. But with enough of these reoccurring experiences, many of these new skills *do* become a concrete reality.

Having achieved this, most people choose to go no further and as a result develop an over-inflated sense of self. However, this seeking only for the sake of visible power is, of itself, self-limiting as it prevents entry to the higher levels which require the letting-go of the Yang forms of strength in favor of the internal Yin power.

The development of Yin power is in many ways the antithesis of the Yang method. The most notable difference is the letting-go of our normal concept of what makes power in the first place.

In order to manifest Yin strength, one must primarily rely on the internal, with the body acting as a conduit. To this end, one may even let go of frame and posture itself in favor of the absolute relaxation and focus necessary to project, affect and control the opponent's Chi.

# MENTAL AND SPIRITUAL DEVELOPMENT

This form of evolution is really a hidden by-product of the practice itself, though it's actual manifestation is dependent upon the consciousness of the practitioner and their willingness to release the desire for power for it's own sake.

Really this is a letting go of one form of power in order to receive something beyond power itself, the expansion of consciousness or what some would call higher awareness.

Once most of the problems of the body have been resolved, one becomes aware that certain other types of changes are taking place. These have to do with Zhan Zhuang's ability to change consciousness.

In simple terms, when the Chi flow becomes strong enough to flood the Central Channel, the Chi rises and interpenetrates the brain. It then begins acting upon the pineal and pituitary glands, which automatically triggers a sympathetic reaction in all the other glands.

Whereas for the development of martial power we concentrate around the navel or low Dan Tien, when we begin to 'grow the Shen,' our arena of focus changes to the upper Dan Tien.

The Zhan Zhuang path to expansion of consciousness comes through a unique interconnected awareness of the body and it's more subtle electromagnetic energies and their relationship to the even more subtle emotional and mental energies.

Many paths to awareness focus solely in the head area. This exaggerated concentration many times causes health problems on the one hand and emotional and mental imbalances on the other.

One of the reasons for this is that when the highest centers open, the flow of energy can be so intense that the unprepared body simply cannot handle it and overloads, causing serious physical, emotional or mental problems and sometimes all three.

Imbalances stemming from such causes are difficult and at best, lengthy to correct.

This is where the Zhan Zhuang method differs. By first strengthening and healing the body and opening its channels naturally, one is at the same time also cleansing and refining the emotions stored in the organs in addition to the nervous system and brain. This cleansing enhances one's mental capacity to cope with increasingly greater and greater flows of power.

So, when quantum leap experiences do occur in our training, while they can temporarily upset and redefine what we consider our balanced state, they do not cause our body or emotions to freak-out or break down in the process.

This is actually the ancient way to enlightenment. That is, one begins with the gross elements and actions of the physical body such as the basic front punch and proceeds to refine all physical motions until they reach a super sensitive balance.

This also means as mentioned earlier that the true understanding of these motions first occurs in the stillness of Zhan Zhuang meditation.

As part of this process, elements of the cellular and emotional memories surface to be reckoned with and resolved. That is why often times, especially in the first few years of training, one may have many emotional ups and downs during a particular session.

The end result of all this is the eventual resolution of the body's major physical, emotional and mental karmic patterns which frees up the individual to go beyond themselves.

This ability to let go and travel beyond one's sense of self is the key to the doorway leading to the higher states. In Zhan Zhuang, these will generally begin with the opening of the three Dan Tiens and the Central Channel.

## THOUGHTS ON SINKING THE CHI

The Classics say that the Chi should sink to the Dan Tien. But what does this really mean? As always there are the three components, physical, energetic and mental. And each of these must ultimately work in congress in order to achieve the desired result. We'll examine the physical aspect first.

Simply put, what we are doing is surrendering to gravity. We do this by first establishing the alignment of the bones and then allowing the muscles and sinews to relax, open up and release, first downward and then outward, accordingly.

A good way to think of this is that the bones are like a coat hanger and the muscles and sinews are the coat hanging on the hanger. The tops of the shoulders and the arms are a perfect example. In the *Wuji* posture they should relax downward just like how a coat hangs.

It is important to note that the coat is supported by the hanger. This means the muscles are supported by the bones, not the other way around. Once we get a handle on this, the stage is set for the gradual connection of all elements of the body's unified structure. This includes the organs, glands, brain and bone marrow.

When the Chi finally 'sinks' what is it that we will feel? Firstly, there is a sense of an expanded connection between the bottoms of the feet and the Earth or whatever you are standing on.

This feeling in the feet can also be felt as a heaviness in that area while at the same time the rest of the body is integrated, light and yet filled with a certain fullness. This fullness is a reflection of the abundance of Chi generated during one's practice. There is also a springy responsiveness felt throughout the body. This can be especially apparent in the muscles, tendons and ligaments.

The first time I felt this in a profound way, I was standing in a Wu Style (Northern Wu) posture. One moment I felt normal and the next it felt as though I had completely bent my knees such that I was very close to the ground.

When I opened my eyes to check, I was astounded to find that my overall posture had only sunk about an inch in total. What I had actually felt was the majority of my Chi descending step-by-step into the ground.

One thing's for sure, the sinking of the Chi cannot occur merely by the use of the will. In fact any amount of over-focusing on such a result will surely keep it from happening.

However, this can often be a fine line because we must use our Yi to center our feeling-awareness in the Dan Tien or the bottoms of the feet in order to achieve the desired result. This follows the principle of, "...the mind leads the Chi."

Here it is useful to adopt the attitude of *Wu Wei* or effortless doing. Simply put, this means centering our attention *without the narrowness of the focus creating tension.* This tension often manifests when the practitioner tries to hold too much of their consciousness in a specific point in the body.

At first, in terms of overall relaxation it is often better to focus and hold the majority of one's consciousness at the location while at the same time allowing a small percentage for peripheral awareness cognition. This means that what we feel will sometimes shift between our focal point and other elements of the body. When this occurs we don't worry about it but simply return our relaxed feeling-awareness to our focal point and continue.

The percentage ratio of our central and peripheral focus, should be determined by the lack of physical tension or stress. As we become more comfortable with the process the ratio will move closer and closer to one hundred percent and zero.

This means eventually one is able to focus their entire consciousness in a single point location to the extent that they become unaware of the physical and feel only their own energy.

In order to do this we must find a way to let go and then let go again and again. This is a letting go of both outward tension and the inward tension of desire. So what does that leave us with?

Hopefully with alignments integrated for full Chi flow and the emotions balanced, in effect, neutral. With a calm and placid mind, we surrender to gravity, also known as the Yang, Heaven or descending energy and trust the Yin, Earth or rising energy to hold us up. In other words, these two forces must balance each other.

When this occurs then not only does the Chi truly sink down into the Dan Tien, through the feet and into the Earth, but an even more refined Essence fills the body from below. This gives one the feeling of both being solidly connected to Heaven and Earth, but also being suspended between them. This is the trinity of Heaven, Man and Earth or *Tian, Ren, Di*.

Once this experience begins to occur on a regular basis then energetically our goal becomes *Wu*. This means that we are operating to create an experience of a greater and greater amount of emptiness or sense of space within the body. This usually starts in the low Dan Tien and then gradually expands until it permeates all of our physical and energetic structures.

Initially, this spacious feeling or insubstantiality is often the result of a quantum factor that can occur when enough physical linkage has been gained such that it generates a response in the energetic bodies. The result can also be feelings of time and space displacement.

# GETTING INTO THE STAND

# ADJUSTING THE SPINE

In Zhan Zhuang there are numerous stances or postures to choose from, depending upon one's goals. Most have specific uses or cultivate various types of energy, but they all have one thing in common. They each utilize what can be called a vertical or 'pine tree' spine.

For the sake of this discussion we will work with the Wuji posture. So how do we create the desired result? In a word what we must do is 'straighten' the spine.

This means minimizing the three curves, the cervical which is naturally concave, the thoracic which is normally convex and the lumbar curve which is customarily concave. What we will be doing is *reversing* the natural direction of these curves in order to create a vertical spine. The following method will get you in the ballpark.

**Sitting On A High Stool**

***Method 1***

1) Assume the basic Wuji posture. Be sure to tuck in your chin.

2) Temporarily straighten your knees and lock them backward.

3) From there, imagine you're going to sit down on a high stool. Picture the stool itself is located in the region of the sitting bones or the crease that separates the buttocks from the back of the thighs.

4) Next, simply 'sit' just enough so your knees *unlock*. The angle of the back of the knee which is nearly 180 degrees when locked is now reduced to let's say 160 degrees or something like that.

### *Method 2*

1) Assume the Wuji posture.

2) Lift your arms straight above your head, palms facing toward each other. Raise them high enough to slightly lift the entire torso, including the Sacrum.

3) Now lightly lock out your legs. Next, while keeping the arms suspended above, unlock the knees and sit ever so slightly as if on a high stool. When done correctly, this move will straighten the lumbar and thoracic curves.

4) Now without sitting any further or collapsing the torso, *slowly* lower your arms. Feel the shoulders settle, then the chest and shoulder blades, the Solar Plexus and the 'mirror' areas on the back and sides.

Next release the waist, lower abdomen and lumbar region. Here one must be extremely careful *not to collapse* the midriff and the area of the Obliques.

This technique is a quick and simple way for even the most seasoned veteran to open the body and drop into a solid meditative state.

The idea is while lowering the arms, we try to release each descending station of the torso, hips and legs all the way down through the bottoms of the feet.

With time, this can be done with much greater detail regarding the release of each section of the body, but for now these two methods will serve as reliable entrées, both for beginners and more advanced practitioners.

It is important to remember that this 'sitting' must always take place from at least the top of the Superior Iliac Crest or better yet from the upper attachments of the Psoas muscles so as to create the 'Hanging Basket Effect' in the torso and Kua. We'll discuss this later.

These two methods work primarily with the thoracic and lumbar curves. For the advanced practitioner, properly tucking in the chin will, of itself reverse the cervical curve and straighten the neck.

For less experienced practitioners, a number of additional adjustments such as the Head and Neck Adjustment Method and the Wuji Spinal Stretch will be found to be most useful.

## WUJI SPINAL STRETCH EXERCISE

The following procedure is a quick way to achieve the necessary spinal alignment. In its basic form it's a relatively simple method suitable for beginners.

At an advanced level this method includes the elements necessary to enter into the proper balance and integration for a deep meditative session. These include, opening and closing, separating and combining and expanding and condensing. At its basic level the exercise is as follows.

**Position 1** - Assume the basic Wuji posture. (see photo sequence)

**Position 2** - Using the top of the hips (the Superior Iliac Crest) as a fulcrum, incline the torso forward while keeping the spine straight. At the same time release the Sacrum, buttocks and legs backward and downward.

**Position 3** - Next, incline the spine a little further forward and while doing so again relax the lower part of the body backward and downward but this time keep relaxing and releasing until you feel your weight sink into your heels.

**Position 4** - At that point the body will have made contact with the Earth energy and will naturally feel the impetus to begin *reversing the incline*. From there, again progressively release downward starting with the hips, buttocks, thighs, calves and feet.

**Position 5** - With each successive downward release the body will be impelled slowly upward until once again vertical.

This is the basic method. The advanced version requires the ability to stretch and condense the tissues of the body at will, without changing or breaking the overall structure.

The outer form of the advanced method is identical to the basic version. Its what goes on under the skin, so to speak, that is more complex. The process for the first three positions is the same as the basic method. It's the rising up from Position 3 into Positions 4 and 5 where things get more complicated.

We'll start from Position 3. *Before* you begin your release and start rising up into Positions 4 and 5, first stretch all the tissue from the Chi Kung Ming Men, the space below the fifth lumbar vertebra and just above the Sacrum, upward into the base of the skull. At the same time, stretch (condense) all the tissue from the bottoms of the feet up into the area of the Chi Kung Ming Men and low Dan Tien. This stretch will have the effect of closing the Kua and this must be done without altering the postural alignment of the bones.

Now as you begin your progressive downward releasing in order to rise up into Position 4, relax the two stretches and then finish as in the basic method. By lifting and condensing first, you have created even more space for the tissue to drop down.

This method fulfills what the Classics say. "If you want to go up, first go down, if you want to go down, first go up." When done properly, the progressive downward releasing causes the torso to rise back up to vertical while opening (lengthening) the entire spine at the same time.

Using these Stations is not the be all, end all however. With enough practice the space between each vertebra of the spine can be individually opened and lengthened.

**Position 1**

**Position 2**

**Position 3**

**Position 4**

**Position 5**

**List of Stations of the Back And Neck**

1) Buttocks
2) Sacrum
3) Lower back
4) Middle back
5) Upper back
6) Cervical spine

The lower back can also be divided into between two and five 'Sub-Stations.' Five being each of the lumbar vertebra.

The middle and upper back and the cervical spine can also be subdivided into smaller Stations and eventually into each of the individual vertebra.

## HEAD AND NECK ALIGNMENT METHOD

The following procedure is an excellent way to align the head and neck correctly. The idea is to take out the curve in the cervical spine.

**Position 1** - Assume the basic Wuji posture. (see photo sequence)

**Position 2** - Make a fist with either hand and then press the back of the wrist under the chin and against the throat.

**Position 3** - Wrap and secure your chin around the inside of the wrist such that if you relax the arm it will still be held in place.

That's how it should feel, but don't actually lower the arm unless you want to test if its secure.

Also, be sure to stretch your chin all the way around the wrist or as much as feels comfortable.

**Position 4** - Now, with the chin tightly wrapped around the wrist, raise your head back up to vertical *without letting go.* If you did it right the cervical spine will be vertical and the curve removed.

**Position 5** - Remove your wrist and press your index finger against *Renzhong* point GV-26, in the cleft of the upper lip below the nose and push the head and neck back slightly.

As you do this be sure to *relax the throat* and keep the *chin tucked in.*

**Position 6** - While maintaining the head and neck alignment you've just created, lower your hand and return to Wuji posture.

One note of caution. When you push back with your index finger, be sure that the chin and head *do not* lift upward. If they do, if the chin sticks out, you must try again because if there is an incorrect lifting, the cervical spine automatically becomes concave again. If this does happen, try keeping your chin more firmly tucked down and in. This usually solves the problem.

There's another trick to this method. When raising the head back up to vertical, allow the rest of the spine and particularly the lumbar spine to relax and also move *very slightly* backward. This helps keep the whole spine correctly aligned.

With this in mind, it is also wise to allow the lumbar spine to move slightly backward a second time when you push your head back with your index finger.

**Position 1**

**Position 2**

**Position 3**

**Position 4**

**Position 5**

**Position 6**

## THE HEIGHT OF THE STAND

There are two ways to approach choosing the right height for one's standing session. Height in this case is dependent on two factors: the amount or angle of one's knee bend and the width of one's stance. For most stances there are basically three heights with many variations.

In the original or traditional method the knees are quite bent, though never further than the base of the toes. The idea behind this is to create a great deal of Chi pressure in the body, especially the lower body.

This amplified Chi then acts much like water from a fire hose, scouring out Chi blockages. It is my understanding that this method is the fastest way to open the body for the development of martial power. This method is definitely a trial-by-fire and as such causes many to give up.

This deep-knee method is certainly not advised for anyone with joint injuries in the lower body. That said, this method can sometimes open things quicker, but for many it only makes matters worse due to being unable to release the requisite tension of their blockages.

A less intrusive approach and the one that I prefer, especially for the novice, is the method used for health and to heal injury. This method is diametrically opposite to the previous.

I refer here to what we call 'tall standing' where one only unlocks their knees rather than actually flexing or bending them. This method is referenced in the Sitting on a High Stool exercise mentioned previously. Although this second method creates less Chi pressure, its great benefit is that it puts a lot less stress on the spine, joints and internal organs.

Also there's another significant factor to this. I've found that as the body does begin to strengthen and heal, one's center of gravity will naturally want to become lower of itself. That is, at a certain point with daily practice, you'll find yourself wanting to bend the knees a little more.

And that desire will feel perfectly natural which means the body will be able to adapt and sustain the greater flexion without too much difficulty.

Therefore the 'tall standing' will eventually produce a middle ground between the knees-unlocked health method and the deep flexion of the traditional martial arts method.

Now that we have discussed the vertical element, the question becomes how does the horizontal aspect effect all this? The horizontal or lateral aspect is defined by the distance between the feet.

In terms of this distance, we have three basic widths: hip width, shoulder width and narrow width.

The general maxim is: The lower and wider you stand, the more you sacrifice vertical movement. The taller and narrower you stand, the more you sacrifice laterally.

Usually it is best to start in the 'middle' or hip width and then get wider over time. Then with *a lot* more practice one moves to the advanced narrower stances for the greatest relaxation and martial agility.

In regard to this evolution the Classics say, "First expand, then contract." The three basic widths will be discussed in more detail later.

## THE LENGTH OF THE STANDING SESSION

The length of one's Zhan Zhuang session can vary greatly. Traditionally one stands about 40 minutes for health and about one hour or more for martial arts power development. That said, for most people starting out, these times should be the goal.

For those who are injured or who are over 50 or 60, it is often important to proceed more slowly. For example, they might start with much shorter times, 10, 15, 20 or 30 minutes depending on one's condition.

But there is a wisdom behind the traditional times. The idea with 40 minutes a day for health is that one must put in enough time daily in order to generate the conditions in the body necessary to instigate healing. This primarily has to do with an increase in the internal Chi circulation.

So for those, who for whatever reason can only hang in there for a short session, simply repeat the shorter time about 2 or 3 hours after the first session or later in the day to get to the 40 minute health mark.

**The Time Factor**

Everyone's body has what can be called a 'time of endurance' or a threshold limit, that is, the length of time the body can bear and endure discomfort or pain. For some this can be the whole length of a traditional standing session. Unfortunately, because of this Spartan ability, these folks are often slow in resolving blockages and other problems simply because they don't know how to let go.

But for most, the body, and generally in the beginning this means the muscles, will reach a point where they just can't seem to go on.

When this happens if we can manage to hang in there a little longer, the effected area will send a message to the brain. The brain in turn will send back a message which causes the whole area to *let go*. When this happens we feel a definite relaxation in the region and also many times, a sense of space or openness.

Sometimes however, if the pain is becoming extreme, the message from the brain might be something like, lower your arms or just stop.

For the Spartan types, these kind of messages are almost subconsciously blocked out altogether or simply ignored through the power of the will or intention. If one looks at this objectively, it is apparent that there is an avoidance or aversion toward really being in touch with their bodies.

But for the rest of us, these signals and sensations can act as important signposts. Though it is true that *Yiquan* translates loosely as 'Intention Fist,' this does not necessarily mean intention without common sense.

Though in truth there are moments when it is appropriate to tough it out, many times depending on one's situation, meaning injuries or structural problems, it is far better to listen to the body and lower your arms. Return to the Wuji posture and rest the overly-fatigued muscles for a little while and then resume the particular arm position.

Any discussion about the length of the standing session would not be complete without addressing the difference between using say eight postures in 40 minutes versus holding just one posture for the whole time.

In my experience both have advantages and disadvantages. Holding multiple postures for short periods has the advantage of alternating between different muscle groups which can reduce the overall stress. In addition, each time you move from one posture to another it alters the emphasis of the overall Chi flow. In many of the postural sequences these changes are very deliberate and are calculated to create a specific overall effect.

On the other hand by only using shorter periods for each posture, the body's 'time of endurance' is seldom reached, making some of the deeper changes slower to come about.

Conversely, by holding one posture for the whole time, one may reach their 'time of endurance' threshold several times and experience a number of openings and deep releases.

The point of all this is to listen to your body and trust in it's innate wisdom. Personally I prefer this 'Taoist style' approach, being natural and dealing with whatever comes up as it happens. This means being willing to be adaptable.

Too much rigidity, in maintaining the perfect posture no matter what, leads to stiffness in martial technique as well as possibly new blockages to go with what one already has.

The idea of 'perfection of symmetry' is somewhat overrated. Just look at nature. No two tree limbs grow exactly alike. Therefore 'perfection of symmetry' should be a goal, albeit one we try to achieve everyday.

But at the same time we must be gentle with ourselves such that we realize and *accept* ourselves just as we are in the present moment, and the next present moment and the next. This way perfection becomes the path not a rigid absolute.

**Mirror Practice**

That said, it's sometimes good to check your posture in front of a full-length mirror. There's an old saying which goes, 'the camera never lies,' meaning because of the objectivity you can't fool yourself.
In this case it's the mirror which will give you an accurate reflection of what's really happening.

Try this: stand in front of a mirror, form the 'Holding the Ball' posture then close your eyes. Stand like that for a minute or two, relaxing as much as possible, then open your eyes. Correct for symmetry while feeling the difference in your relative relaxation then close your eyes and try a second time, again allowing things to relax as best you can.

# NOTE TO OLDER PRACTITIONERS

When a person turns fifty and for every decade thereafter, their body's healing ability incrementally slows down. So if one is dealing with an injury or internal organ problem for example, right off the bat you should know it takes longer to heal and resolve these difficulties.

What used to take a day or two to heal in our thirties can easily take a few weeks or even a month or so in our sixties. Although Zhan Zhuang can mediate this, especially in the case of long-standing practitioners, one must still cultivate a good deal of patience.

A good rule of thumb for the older practitioner is to remember to emphasize much more of the relaxation element rather than too strict an adherence to structural alignment. (Structure vs. Relaxation)

**The Body Wants To Heal**

If you let it, the body knows what to do and will lead you if you surrender to it's 'suggestions.' This means that even if your alignments aren't ramrod perfect, don't judge yourself too harshly.

Over time the body itself will begin to 'suggest' changes and if you let it, initiate corrections. Therefore, it behooves us to cultivate a sensitivity to these mostly subtle impulses.

The body has an innate wisdom if we listen. There's an old saying in Chinese Medicine, "The body wants to heal itself." This means that the main part of our job in each session is just to show up!

If we 'do our time' each day, we will look back after 90 days of daily practice and see, feel and know positive changes that have taken place.

Although we may not yet be able to put them into words, the overall sensations of feeling better will always be a part of the equation.

By the way, this inability to articulate the changes proliferated by Zhan Zhuang is one of the reasons there is virtually no literature describing the details of it's transformation process. Hence, the reason for the present work. And I am no different than any other practitioner, it's taken years to put words to the feelings.

**Be Gentle With Yourself**

So to summarize, the key for older practitioners is to be patient and gentle with themselves and proceed gradually, incrementally.

Use higher, more comfortable stances and most importantly build the length of your daily sessions gradually.

Rather than 'no pain, no gain' being the mantra, the opposite needs to be the case. If there is pain it is a signal from the body that there is a problem which needs to be addressed.

This is not to say that a certain amount of discomfort won't be necessary from time to time as the body acclimatizes, strengthens and heals.

What one needs to develop, and Zhan Zhuang is very helpful in this regard, is *discrimination*. In other words the ability to know the difference between real pain which is a red flag and the various forms of discomfort which are usually the result of the body's adaptive and healing processes.

**Sensitivity To The Chi**

The key to this, especially at the outset, is to trust your intuition. That said, it is wise to remember that everyone's pain threshold is different. In terms of sensitivity to the Chi there are four broad categories: insensitive, sensitive, very insensitive and very sensitive.

Determine which one most closely fits you and act accordingly. If you're on the insensitive side, develop more sensitivity by listening more carefully to the body. On the other hand, if you're oversensitive, perhaps you need to develop some more will power.

# FEET PARALLEL STANCES

# FEET-PARALLEL STANCES

Here we will discuss in more detail the three widths that are generally used with feet-parallel stances and why. They are: hip width, shoulder width and narrow width.

**Hip Width**

The first distance is hip width. This refers to the outsides of the feet being aligned with the outsides of the hip. Specifically the top of the Iliac Crest lines up with *Heding* point just above the kneecap and *Jiexi* point ST-41, between the two tendons in the center of the ankle.

This is the body's natural alignment which some call the Universal Matrix. This width allows the tissue to relax and the alignment of the bone structure to be in the most natural and supportive manner. This is the preferred width when working with injuries.

**Shoulder Width**

The second distance is shoulder width. This means there should be a straight, vertical line from the outside of the shoulder down through the outside of the ankle and foot.

This width is generally used for martial arts power development as it stretches and opens the tissue and strengthens the tendons and ligaments far more than the hip-width method.

There is also a word of warning which goes with the wider (and lower) stances. One must be extremely careful about the alignment of the knees especially at the beginning of this type of practice because often the Kua is not sufficiently open to accommodate the wider width. It is interesting to note that in practitioners with thirty or more years experience, the shoulder width distance will appear to have the same vertical alignment and structural integrity as their hip-width stance. In other words their Kuas have become very open and there's a telltale hollow look to the region.

**Narrow Width**

The third distance, narrow width, is an advanced stance in which the outsides of the feet are placed at distances narrower than hip width.

This position provides the greatest relaxation and agility but requires extra vertical elongation in order to work. The famous photo of *Wang Xiang Zhai* standing outside in his yard is an example of this type of posture.

These type of stances are used for among other things, to further refine our sense of balance and narrow our centerline and Central Channel.

This in turn provides the advanced martial artist with the ability to 'pivot on a dime,' and perhaps even more importantly, to turn their centerline into the thinnest of threads, thereby creating the ability to hide their center from their opponent. The Classics say, "...I know the opponent but he does not know me."

**The Six External Harmonies**

The Six External Harmonies are a series of correspondences throughout the body. They are physical and energetic links between the upper and lower, the arms and legs and various parts of the torso. Here's the simplest breakdown.

1) Shoulders and Hips
2) Elbows and Knees
3) Hands and Feet

This means there is a relationship between these regions of the body as regards their ability to open and close and later, to move together and in direct proportion. These are also some of the fundamental hardwiring connections that need to be instilled in the subconscious in order to fulfill what is stated in the Classics, "...when one part moves, all parts move."

A more detailed breakdown will be of value here. In this case we will start from the spine as the centerline of the body. The description of one side will apply to both.

Starting from the spine we move laterally along the Rhomboid muscles which connect to the shoulder blade. Next, we follow the Teres muscles which link the shoulder blade to the Humerus bone of the upper arm.

From there we move to the shoulder joint itself and then down the Triceps and Biceps muscles of the upper arm to the elbow joint. Finally, we follow the muscles of the forearm down to the wrist, palm and fingers. This describes the integration necessary with the arms.

Simply put, the idea is to go from the spine all the way out to the finger tips when we expand, and from the finger tips back into the spine when we condense.

The lower body follows a similar procedure only now we go from the Dan Tien and Ming Men regions down and out to the bottoms of the feet. The lower route moves laterally from the Ming Men and Sacrum through the buttocks, hips and Kua, down through the hamstrings and thighs and into the knee joints. From there it moves down the calves and shins into the ankles and feet.

This idea of expanding from the center to the extremities as we inhale, and condensing from the extremities into the center on the exhale, mirrors the Universal Pulse, the alternating contraction and expansion, the natural Yin-Yang 'breath' of the universe.

Below is a more complete list of upper and lower correspondences. We begin with the Cranium and the Cervical and Thoracic Spines for the upper harmonies and the Sacrum for the lower.

**External Harmonies - Upper and Lower Correspondences**

| Upper | Lower |
|---|---|
| Spine (up to base of skull) | Sacrum |
| Shoulder Blades | Buttocks and Kua |
| Shoulder Joints | Hip Joints (side of hips) |
| Elbows | Knees |
| Wrists | Ankles |
| Hands | Feet |
| Fingers | Toes |

**Wuji Posture - Hip Width**

**Shoulder Width**

**Narrow Width**

# FEET PARALLEL - LEFT-RIGHT WEIGHTED

After one has spent a considerable amount of time, generally about a year, becoming familiar and comfortable with the basic parallel stances, it is time to branch out and challenge the body a little.

The first and easiest variation of the parallel stances is where we shift a portion of our weight as well as our centerline to one side for a period of time and then to the other for the same amount of time.

Although this appears to be a simple change at first, one immediately finds several factors which need to be addressed. The first of these is the adjustment of the weighting itself.

When one shifts the majority of their weight to one side, the weighted leg is now challenged to take more of the body weight (gravity and Chi pressure) and still be relaxed.

To accomplish this we need to address two factors. The first is the increase in the refined balance necessary to become relaxed on the weighted leg. The second is, what do we do with the less weighted leg? And finally, what is the redefined relationship between the two?

From previous experience in the Wuji posture we know that the body can be divided into three basic vertical sections, center, left and right. We can also think of it three dimensionally as front, back, inside and outside. These apply to the torso and especially the legs.

When we shift the weight more to one side these same factors will come into play, only now in a dimensionally smaller and more subtle way. Let's examine the weighted leg first.

For this example we will utilize the four divisions as our model. Front to back constitutes depth while inside to outside or vice versa, represents width.

If we can become aware of halfway between the front and back of the leg and halfway between the inside and the outside, we can roughly determine a line or plane of intersection which would be equidistant between the four sides.

It is there that we will find our balance point. The fact is, we've found this area already in the basic stances only now the dimensions between each of the two pairs is greatly reduced, hence the need for a more refined balance.

So as we relax and balance ourselves on the more weighted leg, the question becomes what do we do with the less weighted, more elongated side?

By the very nature of having to bear less weight, the elongated side has the potential for greater relaxation through opening and emptying. The idea here is to divide the body in half at the spine.

The key to this is, as you begin to release the Kua, instead of dropping the weight of the elongated side into its attached foot, we channel much of the weight into the weighted side. The less weighted side then begins to feel more relaxed and elongated with only a small amount of additional weight actually reaching the foot.

At an advanced level you can start your release at Dazhui, below the cervical spine. Let's say your left is the weighted side and your right is less-weighted and more elongated. As you release down through the Thoracic and Lumbar spines, allow the laterally elongated tissue to the right of the spine to relax and feel as empty of weight as possible. Any feeling of weight or tension is transferred to the weighted side and directed down under the foot.

At first the best way to do this is to release the spine and attached tissue in sections. From Dazhui to the top of the shoulder blades, From the top of the shoulder blades to the bottom of the shoulder blades, etc. And each time you release a section of the spine make sure the weighted side absorbs any tension so that the elongated side can remain as relaxed and empty as possible.

**Allow The Heart Chi To Descend**

When beginning this practice as part of your daily routine, it is generally best to start with the left side bearing the weight. The reason for this is to allow the Heart Chi to descend first. This is it's natural direction of flow. The Chi in the Heart meridian starts in the armpit and moves downward to the pinky finger.

When training this method we will want to utilize the same three widths as with the equal-weighted stances. (see photos)

Hip width requires only a modest weight-shift and as such is the simplest and least intrusive transition from the basic equal-weighted postures. It is therefore often the best place to start.

Shoulder width is an excellent way to deepen and improve the 'Cloud Hands' motions of any Tai Chi style. Keep in mind when choosing how wide to stand be sure that the distance you select allows a vertical alignment of the weighted leg.

With the less-weighted leg, be sure the knee is clearly unlocked and that the hip bone, kneecap and ankle are all in the same plane.

Also be *sure* the hips are parallel. It often happens that in the act of shifting the weight, the hips will twist slightly. This is usually due to tightness in the Kua or low back.

One way to remedy this is to imagine that you're standing in a very narrow hall, so narrow you can't move forward or backward, only side to side. The idea is to prevent any lateral rotation.

Another method is to rest your Sacrum against a wall and then shift the weight. If there is no hip rotation, your backside should still be touching the wall.

Now we come to the advanced narrow width variation which provides the most subtle refinement of balance. This width is an excellent training for those working with the Sun (Lu Tang) style of Tai Chi. In Sun style the weighting of the legs of their 'Brush Knee' is nearly a hundred percent and zero with the feet almost parallel, after a step-and-slide type of delivery motion.

As with all narrow width stances, it's important to elongate the midriff and spine. Also be sure that the weighted leg is almost completely straight with the knee unlocked but not bent very much.

**Wuji Posture Right-Weighted - Hip Width**

**Right-Weighted - Shoulder Width**

**Right-Weighted - Narrow Width**

## TOE-OUT STANCES

The toe-out stances have a great benefit when compared to their parallel cousins. They markedly reduce stretch in the lower back and hips and as such are useful for those with injuries in those areas.

One can use the same three widths as with the feet-parallel stances. *Wang Xiang Zhai* often used the narrowest version of this method to great effect.

It is interesting to note that some schools of thought believe only in the feet-parallel method because of the balanced equality of energies coming in and going out of the body.

They believe that toe-out stances allow too much of the body's energy to leak out or escape and that the toe-in stances do just the reverse and tend to cut off flow and hold too much energy inward.

In my experience this kind of thinking is erroneous because once we really get our bodies open, we can utilize almost any posture with great result. For example, the 45 degree turnout is used in many standing and fixed-legs Chi Kung methods.

With all three widths, there can be a wide variety of turnout angles. These include 45 degrees, 33 degrees down to just slight turnouts of 5, 10 or 15 degrees.

These latter are recommended for those with tight hips, Kua or lower back and especially those with injuries in those areas. The idea with this is to dip your toe in the water rather than just dive in. In other words, proceed gradually.

There are two important things to remember with the toe-out method. The first is to make sure that both feet are turned out to the *same* angle. While this seems obvious, you'd be surprised how many people lack the natural symmetry due to injury, over-favoring of one side or just plain lifestyle, like too much time at the computer desk. The second thing to be aware of is the alignment of the legs. Here once again we utilize a straight line from the Superior Iliac Crest down through *Heding* point above the kneecap and then down through *Jiexi* point at the center of the ankle. At all costs one wants to avoid the knees being skewed, that is, either collapsed inward or pushed outward.

**Toe-Out Hip Width**

Working with a toe-out stance at hip width takes pressure off the lumbar and sacral regions. It also opens the inguinal region which stimulates the lymph. Later, as one finds a sense of relaxation in the posture, the element of 'splitting' comes in. Splitting is when you feel the tissue on each side of the spinal column open and relax down and away toward the sides of the body. When this occurs there is also a feeling of emptiness in the Central Channel region with the weight being clearly distributed to the left and right legs.

**Toe-Out Shoulder Width**

Standing at shoulder width provides a maximum stretch for martial development, still with a minimum of strain to the lumber region. Also this distance with a 45 degree turnout is the preferred stance for many forms of 'silk-reeling' exercises, common in Chen Tai Chi and certain other styles.

**Toe-Out Narrow Width**

Standing in the narrow version provides for maximum relaxation along with vertical elongation. This facilitates the flow of Intention and power for use with Small Circle attack and defense. And since we often find ourselves standing and waiting in daily life, this narrow version, done with only a very slight turnout, can be adopted while in line at the bank or supermarket. This way without calling attention to yourself, you can turn a boring, mundane experience into a beneficial one.

**The Natural Progression Of Stance Training**

With most all stances and their variations it is often best to start at hip width, sometimes known as normal width. This is generally the most comfortable to begin with. This way we gently allow things to open up before proceeding to the wider shoulder width distance.

The shoulder width variation is often a challenge for many people to do correctly. This is due to the demands made on the body by stretching the deep muscles of the hip, lower back and Kua as well as the tendons and ligaments. If certain areas are resistant or tight, it is easily possible to be pulled out of proper alignment. On the other side of the coin, the benefit to this additional stretching is an overall strengthening of the body's frame and an increased springiness and flexibility in the joints. Try this. Stand at shoulder width for a few minutes and then switch to hip width and realign everything. Notice the increased relaxation and sense of ease in the hips, legs and Kua.

After having passed through the first two stretching stages of the hip and shoulder width distances, we move onto the narrower widths. For this to succeed the body will have had to really open up, otherwise we could find ourselves creating new problems such as lateral compression where the tissues around the spine begin to tighten instead of relaxing and elongating vertically. Just remember, the key to the overall progression is to start in the middle, then expand *and then* condense.

Toe-Out Stance - Hip Width

**Shoulder Width**

**Narrow Width**

## TOE-IN STANCES

Most of the toe-in stances have their origin in the Baguazhang martial art although we also see this stance in Wing Chun's 1st form, *Sil Lim Tao* as well as Goju Ryu's *Sanchin* posture, a number of Southern Style Kung Fu systems and also a few others. This is one of the preferred stances for cultivating the curved or rounded energy found in nature as well as Bagua and Tai Chi.

The toe-in stances are generally the most difficult to get right. This is because by their nature they require the greatest amount of torque and stretch in the low back, hips and knees.

Those with injuries in these areas are well advised to toe-in quite a bit less than the traditional 33 to 45 degrees or in many cases to avoid these postures altogether.

Even so, one must be extremely careful of the alignment of the knees. If the hips and back are too tight, the hips will not be able to properly rotate outward and the result will be that the kneecap will not be angled on the same plane as the ankle, foot and toes. Prolonged standing in this type of misalignment will over time ruin the knees.

In addition, toe-in stances literally pull the tissues of the lumbar region apart. This involves many muscles such as the Quadratus Lumborum, the Gluteus, Sacrospinalis, Piriformis, Psoas, Iliacus, the Iliotibial Band and more. This is virtually the whole Kua.

So, unless you are fully open in the hips and low back, you are well advised to start in the feet parallel stances and then turn the feet in only a little for the first week or so to acclimatize the body.

Then over the next few months, gradually toe-in more and more until you reach somewhere between 33 and 45 degrees.

Please be aware that at the outset this posture does not feel very natural or easy to perform for that matter. Only after a considerable amount of time will one develop sufficient opening to really feel relaxed.

Because the Bagua martial art method requires considerably more stretch and flexibility than Tai Chi or Xingyi, when one does acquire a modicum of achievement with these stances they will feel a sense of openness never previously experienced before.

In addition, to the above mentioned openness, one will also feel a solid, cemented feeling in the legs as if they're being screwed into the ground. This screwing-in sensation is a manifestation of the spiral energy which these types of postures cultivate.

Another great benefit and why these postures are often used, is their ability to also cultivate circular and spherical energy. There is a photo of the complete posture, including arm position on page 334.

One more thing. If you're adding the toe-in method to your overall standing regime, be advised to start with only a few minutes in these demanding postures. Those who do will thank me later. Those that don't, well, unless you're under the guidance of an expert teacher, watch out.

**Toe-In Stance - Hip Width**

**Shoulder Width**

Narrow Width

## FULL AND EMPTY STANCES

This basically refers to any stance where there is more body weight on one leg than the other. These sort of stances cover a wide range from 60/40 back-weighted as in *Xingyi's Santi* posture or the 60/40 front weighted Bow stances of *Chen* Tai Chi to 100/0 as with *Yang* Tai Chi's 'Golden Rooster Stands On One Leg' or the 100/0 Bow stance of *Sun* style Tai Chi. Single-weighted stances per se will be discussed later.

**The Difference in Weight Distribution**
As soon as one leaves the relative comfort of the equally weighted parallel stances, the degree of difficulty begins to mount commensurate with the amount of shift away from 50/50 and toward 100/0.

**A Variety of Widths and Lengths**
With these types of stances the width and length between the feet can vary a great deal, going from the very short as in *Sun Lu Tang's* Brush Knee and Twist Step to quite long and narrow as with many advanced *Yiquan* postures.

In the photo examples shown I have used both short and long, front-weighted Bow stances and back stances, which when cultivated provide greater rooting and integration for all the movements they support.

Remember, as soon as one settles into any unequal weighted stance, the body should automatically divide into a full side and an empty side.

This is a separation of Yang and Yin on a physical level, whereas in the equal weighted Wuji stance, the Yin and Yang will tend to combine. Not to complicate things, but actually this *separating and combining* or 'exchanging' of Yin and Yang occurs throughout each movement of Tai Chi as well as during the stillness of Zhan Zhuang postural meditation.

**The Manifestation of Tai Chi**

In fact as far as Tai Chi Chuan is concerned, it is those brief instants where the Yin and Yang momentarily 'touch' in their process of exchanging, as portrayed in the traditional Tai Chi diagram, that generate what is known as 'Tai Chi' in the first place.

An example of this can be found in the Yang style 'Brush Knee' movement. We'll start with most of the body weight on the back right leg. As we execute the technique, our weight shifts from our back leg to the front left leg as we perform the arm movements.

It is the brief moment when the weight shifting from back to front and from right to left, passes through our centerline that 'Tai Chi' actually occurs.

In addition to their general fullness and emptiness, these types of stances also have an important difference from the feet parallel variety in that they utilize both descending energy, on the rooted side, and ascending or rising energy on the light or empty side. Again this is not to say that this doesn't happen in Zhan Zhuang. The fact is it does, but in a *different* manner.

The general principle is: putting weight on a leg will cause energy to descend while emptying a leg will cause energy to rise. That said, there are exceptions. Aren't there always? In this case I'm talking about the fact that different parts of the foot can cause energy to do different things. We'll discuss this in more detail later.

**Incorporating Zhan Zhuang into a Tai Chi Form**

There are a number of ways to bring our Zhan Zhuang awareness and sense of center into our Tai Chi form. The easiest method is to stand in one or several of the five fundamental postures of *Peng*, *Lu*, *Ji*, *An* and *Dan Pien* - Single Whip.

When we do this all the internal understanding and awareness we have developed in Zhan Zhuang training transfers over and begins to fill the Tai Chi posture. If one persists in this practice, both their external and internal frames will undergo a powerful transformation. This transformation will immediately become evident when we execute the movement in sequence in our Tai Chi form.

Another way to transfer our Zhan Zhuang awareness is to use both the movement of the form and stillness. The method is easy. Begin your form as usual but as you arrive at the 'end point' of each posture, pause, relax and settle in for between one and three breaths. After that proceed to the next movement and briefly pause again and so forth. The end point of a posture is found when our physical expansion has reached its apex.

Both techniques will do wonders in opening your postures as well as greatly improve your sense of center in each particular movement.

I know for some this may seem to violate the principle of 'keep flowing like a river.' But the fact is, there are many, many ways to practice your Tai Chi form. From the standard slow, smooth and continuous to the rippling 'Flag Waving' style that takes only ten minutes to complete and many other kinds of emphasis in between.

**Front-Weighted - Short**

**Front-Weighted - Long**

**Back-Weighted - Short**

**Back-Weighted - Long**

# INITIAL ADJUSTMENTS

## INITIAL ADJUSTMENTS

In this section we will go through the specific regions of the body with an eye to their makeup. This will include the location of a number of masterpoints that have a powerful relaxation effect over large swaths of tissue. So this is a good time to break out the old anatomy book and acupuncture chart or access similar resources online. Please note, the importance of this material cannot be overestimated if one desires serious achievement in either health or internal martial arts.

Before we begin this discussion, it is also important to note that each location has a certain proper way to open. Generally this involves the muscles and fascia elongating and becoming unstuck from the bone. This leads to strengthening of the tendons, ligaments, and attachments.

There are a number of initial postural adjustments that we are wise to consider as we begin our daily session. However, these should be preceded by placing our awareness at *Baihui* point.

**Above the Head, Baihui (Crown) Point**

According to Taoist philosophy, the first thing to become aware of as we initiate our stand is the Heaven energy descending from above. This energy is constantly influencing the body. This is also true of the ascending Earth energy which enters from below through the *Huiyin* point at the Perineum and from under our feet.

At the beginning it is only necessary to become aware of the *Baihui* or crown point and relax the local muscles. This point is found at the intersection of two lines.

The first line is from the apex of one ear to the other. The second is the centerline of the body. Where these to lines intersect, this is *Baihui* point. There is generally a very slight indentation where the point is actually located. *Baihui* point has a notable significance because it is where all the body's Yang Chi meets. It is also an important conduit for the descending Heaven energy. The idea here is to 'open' the point and also to relax and eventually open the various sutures of the skull.

**Head and Neck**

Once we have effectively relaxed *Baihui* point, many of the muscles of the top of the skull will have also relaxed. Allow this relaxation to percolate down over the forehead to *Yintang* point between the eyebrows, the 'third eye.' This point also holds significance, not just for advanced practices but also for its ability to relax the entire body. In China, athletes often have this point massaged or needled before competition due to its superior ability to create a relaxed state both physically and mentally.

Okay, with that in mind, now let the relaxation you've generated spread out across the forehead and into the eyes themselves. Relax the eyelids, the muscles around the eyes and the eyeballs themselves. Finally, focus on the back of the eyeballs where the optic nerve attaches. This area also has a powerful relaxation effect on the entire body. If you work this correctly, the whole body will have ratcheted down in tension.

Let this relaxed feeling spread out to the sides and back of the head, down to the base of the skull and to the muscles of the nose and face. Now focus and relax the muscles around the ear and the ear itself. Pay special attention to the front of the ear in the soft tissue where it 'connects' to the jaw, and in particular, *Tinggong* point SI-19, Palace of Hearing. Also give extra attention to *Yifeng* point TB-17, behind the ear where the jawbone and the skull meet. This area is significant in that it allows the head to feel a 'separation' or 'lifting' off the body. Also, it is intimately connected to the Masseter muscles of the jaw found beneath *Jiache* point ST-6 and *Xiaguan* point ST-7. These are relaxation masterpoints for the lower and upper jaw respectively.

In order to relax the jaw, which helps release deep tension, we must do so while still keeping the tip of the tongue to the roof of the mouth and the back teeth either touching or slightly separated. There's a knack to this which is best experienced by first opening the mouth and jaw and then relaxing the jaw and face muscles as much as possible.

Having felt that, close your mouth, gently rest the back teeth together and place the tip of the tongue to the roof of the mouth. With these alignments in place, now relax the jaw. What you find is a sort of dynamic relaxation with a small amount of tension, compared to the mouth hanging open. This is natural and in fact is present in all of the muscular relationships throughout the body.

Once again, if we relax completely in standing, we fall down. So this is not the relaxation we're talking about. Instead we will use the phrase *Dynamic Relaxation* in order to indicate a certain amount of dynamic tension exists.

Later, this is felt as a greater and greater springiness at which point the idea of tension as tightness, no longer applies. On a side note, there is one area you can and should completely relax and that is the mind. More on this later.

Having relaxed all the muscles of the head and face out to where they attach to the neck and throat, it is time to link and expand our Dynamic Relaxation. We'll divide the neck into three basic parts, the back of the neck, including the cervical vertebrae, the sides of the neck, specifically the Sternocleidomastoid muscles and in front, the throat.

Loosen the muscles at the back of the neck from *Feng Fu* point GV-16 at the base of the skull down to *Dazhui* GV-14 in the space below the 7th cervical vertebra. It is important to point out that here, as well as with most areas of the body, there are several sets of muscles involved. Generally there are three groups at progressively deeper depths, although occasionally there are more or less. With enough practice you will be able to differentiate many of these and relax them.

At the beginning pay particular attention to where the neck muscles originate from the base of the skull and the back of the jaw. Also, to where they join the torso at the top of the shoulders.

The side of the neck also involves several layers of muscles. The most important of these and what we'll mainly work with are the Sternocleidomastoid muscles which are critical to opening the cervical vertebrae and elongating the neck. These muscles also help create the feeling of the head being light and suspended above the neck and torso. The 'SC' muscles are first stretched from the *bottom up*. Then from where they attach behind the ear, they are relaxed downward along with the surrounding tissue, while still maintaining the feeling of a relaxed vertebral extension. (tall neck)

Before we move on to the throat, there is a another set of often troublesome muscles called the Scalenes. These, and there are three, are located on the lateral region of the neck and connect the neck to the shoulder tops and also the upper most ribs. Again while maintaining an upward feeling, relax and release the Scalenes down and into the shoulder tops, upper back and upper chest.

Moving on to the throat. The throat is also composed of three general regions, the center, where the windpipe is, and the soft tissue lateral to the windpipe and medial to the SCs and Scalenes on each side.

Again concentrate and loosen the upper attachments located in the soft tissue high up under the chin and jawbone. Then release these muscles downward to their lower attachments at the clavicle and the all important 'Throat Notch.'

The Throat Notch is the region through which the Chi descends into the chest and abdomen. This is the same path as in Microcosmic Orbit meditation. In addition, when this area opens, one's ability to communicate also improves. This point is often used by Chi Kung experts to bend long steel rods in demonstrations. When one has enough Chi to do this, then the area is protected from certain kinds of blows or strikes.

Note that as we proceed down through the body, especially into the torso, the order of release can vary. The general idea at the beginning is to always go from top to bottom. When you become familiar with all the various regions, you can imagine something like warm water being poured over and through your body from the top of the head down to the bottoms of your feet. Wherever the water goes, your body relaxes.

**The Shoulder Girdle and Shoulder's Nest**

Now we move on to the Shoulder Girdle which is composed of five sections: Front, Back, Outside, Top and Inside.

The front region is often called the Shoulder's Nest and consists of the soft tissue below the clavicle in the area around *Zhongfu* LU-1 and *Yunmen* LU-2 on each side of the upper Chest. It also includes the Pectoralis Major muscles and *especially* the Pectoralis Minor. The Pectoralis Minor is significant for two reasons. The first is its ability to keep the chest relaxed downward or sunk as we raise our arms. The second is its connection with the Subscapularis muscle on the inside of the shoulder blade. This linkage allows the downward release of the

Pectoralis Minor attachments deep inside the Shoulder's Nest to create a similar effect on the shoulder blade. Simply put, releasing the front also releases the back.

And this symbiotic relationship also works the other way around, that is, by releasing the Subscapularis and shoulder blade you also release the Pectoralis Minor, in effect sinking the chest and keeping the shoulder down. Releasing the back also releases the front.

The back region of the Shoulder Girdle refers to the shoulder blade area and includes the Trapezius, Subscapularis, Rhomboids, Levator Scapulae and Teres muscles. We'll discuss these in more detail shortly.

The outside section of the Shoulder Girdle refers to the region of the upper (anterior) Deltoid around *Jianyu* point LI-15 and surrounding tissue. *Jianyu* is a masterpoint for releasing the Deltoid. It also has a great effect on our 'lifting strength' and the transfer of power from the torso out to the arms and hands.

The top section refers to the Trapezius muscle on top of the shoulder and particularly LI-16 *Jugu* point in the depression where the clavicle meets the outer edge of the shoulder blade. Opening *Jugu* point helps create space between the chest and upper back.

And lastly, the inside section is located in the armpit area, including *Jiquan* point, HT-1. Properly opening *Jiquan* has an amazing effect on releasing the whole shoulder girdle thereby keeping our shoulders down as we use our arms. Because of the shoulder's great range of motion, all these regions must be balanced and released carefully, paying attention to how the change in one section effects the others. The importance of this fact cannot be overestimated.

**Dazhui Point**

Next we come to the location known as *Dazhui* GV-14, or the 'Big Vertebra,' on the centerline of the neck, in the depression below the 7th cervical vertebra. The first thoracic vertebrae just below this space will feel quite pronounced, hence the name. *Dazhui* is a masterpoint for the neck and upper back. Physically, the base of the neck muscles attach either directly or in the vicinity. As for the shoulders, parts of the Trapezius and Intercostal muscles also attach there as well as a number of others.

Just as important as the muscle connections, perhaps even more so is *Dazhui's* energetic significance. It is a vital transmission station for nerve messages into the neck and head and also serves a similar function to the shoulders and arms. It's effect can be felt in both the Macrocosmic Orbit meditation and the Chi transmission of Fa Jing.

This is born out in acupuncture when a needle is inserted into the point and heated with moxa. The heat spreads out across the shoulder tops as well as into the neck. With long enough application one often feels the heat continue down to their hands.

**Upper Back, Shoulder Blades**

Next we will consider the muscles of the upper back and shoulder blades and also their connection with the shoulders, chest and thoracic regions.

The outermost muscle group in the upper back is the large Trapezius muscle. Deeper beneath are the Rhomboids, Major and Minor and the Levator Scapulae, the muscle that connects the shoulder blades to the neck. The Rhomboids are often overlooked, but are usually the source of blockage or tightness that so many experience during raised arm postures. You may also find a similar tightness in the Teres Major and Minor muscles which link the shoulder blade with the Humerus bone of the upper arm. There are even deeper muscles, such as the Infraspinatus and the Serratus Posterior which will eventually need to be addressed. These generally have to do with structural adjustments.

Lastly, we have the Subscapularis on the anterior of the shoulder blade, and upper Intercostal muscles, the muscles between the ribs. Many of these deep muscles can be considered as stabilizing muscles which help hold our structure together. Using a long exhaling breath is a good way to make contact with these deeper structural muscles in the torso.

At this point I will briefly mention the two basic muscle-function types. Some have nick-named them *Mobilizers*, muscles which we use to move, and *Stabilizers*, muscles which maintain our structural integrity. A number of muscles fulfill both functions. And this number will increase as our body integration develops until we get to the point where, as the Classics say, "...when one part moves, all parts move."

**Chest, Thoracic Region**

Now we move on to the 'mirror' or opposite region in the front of the body. Here we'll release the Pectoralis Major and Minor muscles from under the Clavicle and after that go deeper and find the Internal Intercostals and Serratus Anterior. Here again, use the breath to help make contact with these deeper, structural layers.

The muscles of the chest consist mainly of the Pectoralis Major and Minor and the Intercostal muscles. The Pectoralis Minor should be of note because when correctly relaxed, it also influences the release of the scapulae. These releases are for the most part vertically oriented, but with some lateral expansion as well. The Intercostals are the muscles between the ribs which stretch and condense as we breathe. As such, they are an important factor in our natural ability to generate

*Kong Chi* (Air Chi) and have it circulate properly. The Intercostals can be thought of a little differently. Though there is the usual vertical releasing, meaning the distance between the ribs, there is also an equally important horizontal or lateral expansion that when fully activated will often fill the front, sides and back of the torso, creating a sort of cylindrical effect.

In addition to the Intercostals, this lateral stretch must also include the cartilage that connects the ribs to the sternum. This tissue can also be opened, albeit only slightly, but certainly enough to feel it.

Lastly, we effect a downward release of the tissue covering the sternum. When this occurs the chest becomes slightly concave, which further rounds and opens the upper back. Pay particular attention to *Shanzhong* point CV-17, on the centerline of the body, on a line, level with the nipples. This powerful point is the home of the body's Ancestral Chi and the middle Dan Tien in Taoist alchemy. It is renowned for it's ability to directly effect respiration and circulation and in particular, the Pericardium itself and therefore the Heart.

**Mid-Back**

Now we move on to an often ignored area, the mid-back. This region starts at the bottom tip of the shoulder blades and goes down to the floating ribs. It's mirror area in front includes the Hypochondrial region located over the Liver, Pancreas and Spleen and the all important Solar Plexus, a control region for the Sympathetic and Parasympathetic nervous systems.

When the muscles of the mid-back are properly released, we often feel a concrete linkage or connection between the shoulders and upper back and the low back, Kua and hips. The mid-back muscles include the Latissimus Dorsi, which begins narrowing toward the spine in this region. In addition there are also the Intercostals and the deep Serratus muscles, off to the sides.

**Solar Plexus and Diaphragm**

The mirror area of the mid-back, the Hypochondrial region and the Solar Plexus bear close examination. The Hypochondrial region follows the contour of the lowest rib in front and includes the tissue just above and below it, all the way to the beginning of the sides of the body.

This region includes the diaphragm, the free movement of which is critically important both to proper breathing and the massaging of the organs that accompanies it. It is also this location and the area just below it, where Chi can become stuck as a result of incorrect practice.

That brings us to the Solar Plexus, home of the twin aspects of the Autonomic nervous system, the Sympathetic and Parasympathetic systems. These are the parts of the nervous system that are under our conscious control (the Sympathetic) and those which are not, the Parasympathetic.

The Parasympathetic system governs such things as respiration, heartbeat, organs and glands, which are not normally available to conscious control. But this doesn't necessarily hold true in all circumstances such as with Yogis or other extremely advanced practitioners. It is our Sympathetic and Parasympathetic nervous systems which undergo changes as a result of the transformation of the nerves which occurs over many years of Zhan Zhuang training.
The other important relationship here is between the Solar Plexus and the Heart and Stomach. In acupuncture, there are points available in this area, on the Ren Meridian, such as *Juque* CV-14 which effect both organs. Another example of this is the old 'knot in the pit of the

stomach' which occurs in this area and is related to both the emotions (Heart) and the physical. (Stomach)

**Midriff**

This area is best described as the tissue from the floating ribs down through the top of the hipbone. It is this region that must be fully elongated and expanded in order to integrate the torso, chest and abdomen with the hips and Kua.

It is also important to note that right below, and in front of the floating ribs are two extremely important points. Below the free end of the 12th rib is GB-25 *Jingmen* (Jing Gate) the *Mu* point (mother point) and Alarm point of the Kidneys. Just to the front of the tip of the 11th floating rib we find LIV-13 *Zhangmen*, the Alarm point of the Spleen, the Assembling point of the Solid Organs and Meeting point of the five Yin Organs.

As you can see, this is a nasty region to strike in a self-defense situation. With sufficient sharpness, power and the correct vector angle of delivery, serious and immediate damage can occur. This could take the form of a massive Chi disruption, a broken rib or the rib detaches altogether and punctures an organ. So be really careful. Also, this region contains the intersection of the External and Internal Oblique muscles which play a critical role in opening and linking the torso.

**Abdomen**

Now we come to the all important abdominal region. For the sake of discussion I will divide the abdomen into two sections. The first will be from the diaphragm to approximately the navel and the second will go from the navel to the Pubic bone, although energetically they are clearly interconnected.

Internally, the upper region houses the stomach, intestines and a lot of sensitive nerves. Covering the organs are a series of tissues and muscles. Going from the inside out they are: Transversus Abdominis, Internal Obliques, Rectus Abdominis and External Obliques. Some of these muscles are also covered with a tendinous sheath in numerous places.

In order to correctly release all of the above, we must become familiar with their various shapes and points of attachment. Look these up in your anatomy text or online reference. A basic working knowledge of the layout of this area will later be invaluable in facilitating the proper execution of opening and closing.

Suffice it to say, most of the release we're looking for is downward, relaxing the tissue from the diaphragm and bottom of the ribs.

After the initial vertical release we encounter the Obliques whose release is somewhat different in that there must be a strong lateral opening, essentially from the centerline out to the sides of the body. But that's not all.

The Obliques are tricky in that there needs to be a *slightly upward movement* of the Internal Obliques and a downward counter-motion from the External Obliques. This element is linked to the lateral movement. One more thing about the Obliques and the midriff and this is important. The ability to move the Obliques in contrary motion actually initiates the proper integration of the upper torso with the lower. Some people call this region the Chi Belt and it is generally a weak area in many practitioners. The good news is, once you gain this achievement and the midriff and abdominal tissue feels a little taut like a drum skin, you've taken a major step toward whole-body integration and strengthened your organs, especially the Kidneys, in the process.

**Lower Abdomen**

The region from the navel to the Pubic bone is of course, inseparable from the rest of the abdomen. Beneath the lower Rectus Abdominis muscles are the Bladder and Prostate Gland in men or the *Bao* or Uterus in women. In addition, the Inguinal region is a primary location of the lymph, so essential to the healthy functioning of the body. If you've ever been a dancer or a martial artist who did high kicks, then you know the importance of opening the tissue in this location which includes most of the *Kua*. If not, then this is an area which will require a good period of time to differentiate, relax and open. Having this region flexible, grounds one's Jing and further increases its power.

Here I want to digress a moment and say something about the location of the Bladder. Besides it's obvious purpose, the Bladder is also the area through which a small amount of pre-natal Chi stored in the *Ming Men*, passes into the Kidney meridian and rises up and is grasped by the Lungs, mixing with the Kong Chi we inhale, *on every breath.* So this part of the abdomen actually effects the quality of our breath.

Energetically, this area is of course, the home of the low Dan Tien, our physical power center as well as our center of gravity. In addition, at the bottom and sides of this region are where many of the tissues of the leg and hip attach. Understanding the relationships of the muscles in this location will greatly expedite the opening of the Kua.

Now we will turn our discussion of the lower Abdomen to two important locations that are often neglected. These focal points are found on a horizontal line, level with the navel, in the indentation where the Rectus Abdominis and the Obliques meet. Sometimes these points are known as the Dan Tien's of the Left and Right Channels. Besides their role in certain alchemical meditations and their ability to open up space between the abdomen and the back, these locations are also significant because they are the exact places that should be *very slightly* withdrawn or held in during Zhan Zhuang practice. Doing this has a number of purposes including establishing the differentiation of movement between the Rectus and the Obliques as well as helping to direct the breath into the Kidneys and low back. Once the breath reaches these areas, the confirmatory sign is an incredible sense of ease or feeling of effortlessness.

**Lower Back and Sacrum**

This region encompasses the tissue from just below the lowest rib, down through the tailbone and includes both the acupuncture and Chi Kung *Ming Men* points, the tops of the hipbones, Sacrum and buttocks as well as portions of the sides of the hips. The acupuncture *Ming Men* point is located in the space below the second lumbar vertebra while the Chi Kung *Ming Men* is found in the space between the fifth lumbar vertebra and the top of the Sacrum.

The low back and Sacral regions also include numerous connections to the *Kua* and are complex in that the sinew attachments and directions of muscle movement are very diverse. That said, proper development and opening of these regions is absolutely essential to any real achievement in Zhan Zhuang. For example, loosening the Sacrospinalis muscle, the muscle that covers the Sacrum, not only helps open the entire region, it also promotes the free flow of Chi and Cerebrospinal fluid up the spine.

Another important set of deep muscles in this region are the Quadratus Lumborum which attach to the spine, the low ribs and the hipbones. These muscles provide much of the lower back's deep, stabilizing strength. When one finally gets a handle on these and gets them to relax and become flexible, the power of their *Jing* jumps exponentially. These muscles have both a clear vertical and horizontal opening.

Lastly, we come to a whole slew of narrowish vertical muscles such as the Spinalis Dorsi, Semi-Spinalis Dorsi, Longissimus Dorsi, Multifidus and the Erector Spinae. These muscle groups all have their origin in the low back, many of them extending almost the entire length of the torso. Opening and lengthening the Erectors for example, is an essential skill needed to control the spine; such as in creating the compression and expansion necessary to 'bend the bow and shoot the arrow.'

**The Spine**

The spine is a most complex mechanism which plays an important, even critical role in the achievement of better health and provides a fundamental element, the 'spring' power necessary for serious internal martial power.

Have you ever seen any of those old black and white formal Chinese portrait photos from the early 20th century? The first thing one notices is how straight-backed the participants are, sitting in their chairs. Spines as straight as pine trees, as the saying goes and of course this is what happens from a dedicated course of standing meditation.

Even a cursory look at the spine shows that there are three curves, the cervical curve, the thoracic curve and the lumbar curve. When we set up for our stand, one of our first jobs is to adjust the body so as to eliminate these curves or at least lessen their concavity if you're just starting out. The goal of course is to create the 'pine tree' spine which actually has an embedded convex element that is used to great effect in Fa Jing.

In terms of health, since every internal organ and body system is connected to the spine through the nerves, the constant stress placed around the areas of greatest concavity can, over time, produce a stagnation of Chi and a weakening of circulation in the ancillary internal systems. Many of these signs have been written off in the West simply as 'aging.' But it doesn't have to be that way.

The reason we start at the top of the body and release downward is so we can use gravity to assist our work. But gravity is really both friend and foe. As a friend, it assists the openness created above to percolate downward. As a foe, it creates unwanted compression over the years.

Ever noticed how when people reach a very old age they seem to have shrunk. Naturally, this unwanted compression puts additional stress on the body and generally creates further health issues.

So you can see the importance of 'straightening' the spine in the fight against time to preserve health and flexibility. This is where Zhan Zhuang becomes a most valuable tool. I once saw an x-ray of the hip of a 90 year old Tai Chi Master, who also trained Zhan Zhuang. According to the doctors, the hip looked like a man in his forties.

**The Curious Case of the Psoas Muscles**

The Psoas muscles cut through the body from back to front. They attach in the upper lumbar region, dropping down and toward the front of the lower abdomen in the area of the Inguinal Crease. For most people, these muscles are heavily engaged when they squat or during sex. Of course they also figure prominently in walking and provide a linkage through the Chi Belt, midriff area, not only in a vertical direction, top to bottom, but also three-dimensionally from back to front and vice-versa.

The Psoas muscles give nearly everyone problems, for two reasons. One, often the length of the left or right Psoas is shorter due to injury or habit. And two, due to their deep location and vectors, they become stuck to surrounding tissue, especially the Quadratus Lumborum. What is curious and unusual about the Psoas is the direction of their release which, in addition to the typical vertical direction also has, and this is critical, an even more important release from front to back.

This is most easily felt by laying on your back with your knees bent and feet parallel. Find a flat surface, the rug for example, Use a thin rolled-up hand towel to support the base of the skull. Rest your palms in the Inguinal Crease. Then just breathe. Abdominal breathing is best.

After a little while you should notice that more and more of your back is touching the surface you're lying on, or sinking in more deeply. The more you can let gravity relax the abdominal muscles and let them sink toward your backbone, the more the Psoas muscles unwind and open.

**The Kua and Hanging Basket Effect**

When one has put in enough time and sufficiently opened the body, it becomes possible to create a feeling of pelvic suspension or the 'Hanging Basket Effect.' The basket is the Kua and what it hangs from is the Psoas and surrounding muscles.

When done correctly one feels almost a floating effect in the Kua and a sensation of great ease while at the same time there is a solid energetic connection and root. The effect itself is primarily based on the ability to elongate the Psoas muscles and relax them towards the back, along with the Quadratus Lumborum, the muscles of the buttocks and the sacral region. This is basically the Kua, the front of which can be defined as from the top of the Iliac Crests to the Pubic bone, including the inguinal creases and the attachments of all the thigh muscles.

The back part of the Kua consists of the Sacrum, buttocks and all the tissue surrounding the posterior hip bones on down through where the

Hamstrings, Adductors, Abductors and other muscles attach. In the West this region might be called the Pelvic Girdle which in terms of the bones, consists of the Ilium, Ishium, Pubis, Sacrum and Coccyx.

**Hips and Buttocks**
The muscles of the hips and buttocks are numerous and if that weren't enough, they attach at many different angles and to many places on the hip bone and around the head of the Femur. The elongation of the hips, especially the side of the hips, which also includes the three Gluteus muscles, plays an important role in creating space for the Hanging Basket effect.

Lining the anterior or inside region of the hip bone are the Iliacus muscles. When these muscles are tight or stuck one can have rotation difficulty as well as stiffness in the hip and low back. Opening these muscles helps make space in the hips, lower abdomen and even the low back. The all-important Psoas Major and Minor muscles also have their lower attachments to the Femur and Pubis bones in this sector. Moving on to the posterior region, we find the muscles of the buttocks which consist of the three gluteal muscles; Gluteus Maximus, Medius and Minimus along with the deep hip rotators, the Piriformis, Gemellus, Obturators and Quadratus Femoris muscles.

The Piriformis muscle which connects the Femur and Sciatic Notch to the Sacrum, is often involved with pain or tightness issues in the lower back and hip. These deep muscles also extend through parts of the lateral region of the hip and buttock. More toward the surface, we find the Tensor Fasciae Latae and the Iliotibial Tract, the tendinous sheath which extends down the upper leg. The flexibility of these tissues contribute to the 'hinges' of the Hanging Basket and account for an important part of the springiness necessary for effective Fa Jing.

**Upper Leg**

Many of the thigh muscles have their attachments in the lowest sectors of the torso. This is the region where tissues connect around the Inguinal Crease and sitting bones and is considered part of the Kua.

The upper leg is divided into four regions, the front, back, inside and outside, also known as anterior, posterior, medial and lateral. It is here one often finds blockage. This region is a key to integrating the lower extremities with the torso in order to create the whole body linkage necessary in Zhan Zhuang and Tai Chi.

In the anterior region we have the Quadriceps Femoris, the Great Extensor muscle of the leg, which consists of four parts. The Rectus Femoris, Vastus Lateralis, Medialis and Intermedius. Together, all these help extend the leg and flex the thigh as well. *These are often the muscles that get sore when we first begin extensive standing practice.* To this end, I would like to introduce a masterpoint that can relax a large portion of the front thigh. The deep point I'm referring to is *Biguan* ST-31. This point is found at the intersection of a vertical line descending from the tip of the Iliac Crest and a horizontal line, level with the Perineum. It's just lateral to the narrow Sartorius muscle which runs from the top of the hip to the medial side of the knee. Opening *Biguan* point will send energy down through the knee into the foot and help relax and link the thigh, buttocks and even parts of the low back.

Continuing on to the lateral region, we find the Tensor Fasciae Latae and the Iliotibial Band. These are the tissues that give the side of the hip and thigh it's solid stability. Releasing them roots the Chi and links the thigh to the lower leg, ankle and foot. These muscles also help flex, abduct, and rotate the thigh along with the Pectineus, the Adductor Longus and the Gracilis muscles.

The posterior region of the thigh is the location of the hamstrings which primarily consist of the Biceps Femoris, Semimembranosus and Semitendinosus. Tightness in this location is often linked with lower back problems. Once again there is a masterpoint which will pretty much release the entire area. This point is *Yinmen* BL-37 and is located about halfway between the crease where the buttocks join the thigh and the crease of the knee, along the centerline of the back of the thigh. Opening this point not only relaxes the back of the thigh but also effects the knee, hip and low back.

**Knee Joint**

The most important thing to know about the knee is that it should not bear excessive weight, but rather transfer it from the hip to the ankle. The key to balance in the knee joint is *Weizhong* point BL-40/ BL-54 in the dead center of the knee, halfway between front and back and halfway between the inside and the outside. This point is accessed from the crease of the knee in back. In Chinese Medicine, *Weizhong* is also considered the Command Point of the lower back. This correspondence reflects the mother and child relationship between the Kidneys and the knees. When this point is opened, the weight from the torso and hips is almost automatically distributed and passed through correctly. The other important location in the knee area is *Heding* point, just above the top of the kneecap. It is through this location that all the combined weight from the front and middle of the body passes down into *Weizhong* point in the center of the knee on its way to the ankle and foot. The critical thing to remember is to *avoid stress through the kneecap.* At the beginning, if there is any doubt, take the weight more through the back half of the knee and calf regions rather than too much in the shins. Weight from the back of the knee spreads out into the heel, whereas weight from the front of the knee is disseminated into *Yongquan* K-1 and the big and little balls of the foot.

**Lower Leg**

Once the body weight has been transferred through the knee, en route to the ankle it passes through the lower leg. This is the area from below the Patella or kneecap to the top of the ankle. Like the thigh, it also consists of four regions.

In front, we have the Tibialis Anterior, Extensor Digitorum Longus, Extensor Hallucis Longus and the Fibularis Tertius Muscles. These are some of the muscles that stop forward motion, like when a sprinter lets up after a dash. They also work in concert with the thighs and calves as part of our front-back balance.

Located on the lateral side of the lower leg are the Peroneus Longus and Brevis muscles. This pair provides a great deal of lateral stabilization for our lower structure, along with the Tensor Fasciae Latae on the side of the thigh. The masterpoint for this region is *Yanglingquan* GB-34, found in front and below the head of the fibula bone about a hand's distance below the crease of the knee. *Yanglingquan* is also an all-important masterpoint for the nerves and sinews, not just locally, but throughout the entire body.

In the posterior region we find the calf muscles or Gastrocnemius, as well as the Soleus and Plantaris. It is through these muscles that all the weight from the back half of the body must pass. And just as the thighs stop us from falling backward, the calves stop us from falling forward.

The masterpoint for the calves is *Chengshan* BL-57, located in the center of the Gastrocnemius muscle where the two heads meet. Releasing this point will send body weight plummeting into the ankle and heel. It will also have the effect of relaxing a portion of the Perineal region at the bottom of the torso.

But there is an even deeper set of muscles in the posterior region of the lower leg which play an important role in fine tuning our balance in Zhan Zhuang meditation. They are the Tibialis Posterior, Flexor Digitorum Longus and Flexor Hallucis Longus.

Located directly behind the tibia or shin bone and deep beneath the calf, the Tibialis Posterior can provide for the finest refinement in our relaxed standing balance. And the taller and narrower we stand in advanced practice, the more this muscle comes into play.

**Ankle**

The ankle also consists of four regions. To the outside is the Lateral Malleolus and on the inside is the Medial Malleolus. These are the ankle bones. Around and below the Medial Malleolus are points important to the health of the Kidney, while around the Lateral Malleolus on the outside, are significant Bladder points which also effect the back.

In addition, two of these points, *Zhaohai* K-6 and *Shenmai* BL-62, serve as the origin points for the Yin and Yang Heel Channels which function as overseer entities for large, grouped quantities of Yin and Yang Chi. *Shenmai* and *Zhaohai* are also masterpoints used to release the body's weight below the ankle and into the foot and ground.

In the front portion of the ankle we are concerned with the Stomach point *Jiexi* ST-41, on the crease of the ankle, between the two tendons. This masterpoint is a central location for the distribution of all the body's weight throughout the feet. It is also the region where the weight divides between the front or dorsum of the foot and the heel. Another thing to be aware of is the narrowness of the ankle, when compared to the thigh or calf.

This is significant in that this condensation requires a more refined balance in order to successfully pass the weight equally into all parts of the foot.

**Foot**

The four sections of the foot consist of the dorsum or top of the foot, the inside region, the outside region, and the bottom of the foot including the heel. The Stomach, Gall Bladder and Liver meridians pass through the top of the foot while the Spleen meridian traverses the inside region. The Bladder meridian descends along the outside region and the Kidney origin point, *Yongquan* K-1, is found on the bottom of the foot. The foot will discussed in greater detail in the sections, 'The Bottoms of the Feet are the Benchmark' and 'The Five Points of the Foot.' The main thing to know at this point is that the feet are where the sum total of the body's weight must pass into and through, in order to connect to the Earth to form our root.

**The Upper Extremities**

Having already discussed *Dazhui* point, the tops of the shoulders, the shoulder nests and shoulder blades, it's time to turn our attention to the upper extremities. As with the other regions, it is important to become familiar with the origin and end point attachments as well as the 'bellies' of the various muscles. With the upper extremities, it is the release of the tissue above, meaning the shoulder girdle, that makes space for the arms to open locally.

**Upper Arm**

The upper arm consists of the muscles surrounding the Humerus bone. These primarily include the Deltoids, Teres, Triceps and Biceps. Once the Deltoids and Teres muscles are relaxed, the attachments of the Triceps and Biceps have space to elongate. The idea is to have this elongation spread into the belly of the muscles, then continue on down to their points of attachment in the elbow joint region. A good way to test this elongation is to stand in the Single Hand *Peng* posture from Yang style Tai Chi and have a partner slowly push on the forward arm. If done correctly, the Biceps and Triceps should remain relatively relaxed while you root the force.

You or your partner can confirm this by simply touching the upper arm to see if there's any tension. Remember, for proper rooting to occur, the force should be directed down the front of the body, the Central Channel and the back, then down under the feet.

**Elbow Joint**
Once the muscles of the upper arm have relaxed, space is created to open the elbow. But unlike the upper arm, in order to fully open, the forearm muscles, especially their attachments in the elbow joint region must also be elongated.

This elongation starts where the attachments of the upper arm connect to the elbow and follows the change in angle from the Humerus bone to the Radius and Ulna of the forearm. Please note that if the elongation changes the angle between the bones, there is probably overstretching. As a general rule, vertical elongation follows the angles of the bones and extends, but does not alter the original, natural angles. By opening the elbow joint, we also activate the significant acupuncture points located throughout.

In the anterior region, around the crease of the elbow are the deep *He*-Sea points of the Lung, *Chize* LU-5, the Pericardium *Quze* P-3 and the Heart, *Shaohai* HT-3. Opening them enhances circulation and respiration. These points are also capable of storing and transmitting a great amount of fire Chi used in certain types of Fa Jing strikes.

Toward the lateral side of the elbow we find the points *Quchi* LI-11 and two inches down the forearm, *Shousanli* LI-10. This area is largely responsible for our grip strength along with *Tianjing* point TB-10 at the back of the elbow. The proof of this is that if someone makes a punching fist and you sharply strike *Shousanli* point, the tightened fist will open or at least all the power in it will collapse.

On the medial side of the elbow we find the 'funny bone' and the specific location of *Shaohai* HT-3. *Shaohai* is also significant because it is a 'water point' on a 'fire channel'. The Heart energy is considered fire. Opening and releasing the water point can vent excess Heart fire energy which can build up during certain types of Fa Jing practice. It can also be used to vent deep, excess heat after Zhan Zhuang practice, although the points in the palm are generally more useful.

**Forearm**

Now we come to the sinews of the forearm. This region is composed of twenty muscles, eight on the anterior side and twelve on the posterior side. Many of these vertically span the entire region from the elbow to the wrist. The ability to elongate these muscles is critical to the proper opening of the wrist and hand. Besides the grip strength points on the upper forearm mentioned earlier, there are two points on the lower part of the forearm that we should be aware of. These are *Waiguan* TB-5 on the posterior side, two inches above the wrist crease in the center and its mirror point *Neiguan* P-6, on the anterior side. *Waiguan* means Outer Gate. This is a major point for the transmission of Chi and power into the hand and fingers. In fact many tendons associated with the fingers have their insertion points in the region. Test this for yourself. Place your hand on a flat surface, palm down. Locate *Waiguan* point, about two inches above the wrist crease in the center between the Radius and Ulna bones. Press firmly on the point until you feel a dull ache. Now, move each of your fingers one at a time. The connection will immediately become apparent. Now lets address *Neiguan* or the Inner Gate, the mirror point on the anterior of the forearm. This point can have a powerful effect on the Heart, Pericardium and circulation. This location is also a set-up point for *Dim Mak* or spot-hitting strikes.

One last thing regarding the forearm. The elongation of this region is very much dependent upon the proper opening of the shoulder and elbow joints above it. At the beginning, while becoming familiar with the various locations, it is best to relax each region in sequence, one after the other. For example, we open the shoulder blade, then the shoulder, then the upper arm, the elbow, the forearm, etc. We call this one after another method, 'Snaking.' Like the movement of each segment in a snake's body. This is the introductory technique to actualize familiarity. But once this has been internalized, one no longer segments and instead, activates all the regions simultaneously.

**Wrist**

In terms of both Zhan Zhuang and Fa Jing, the wrist is one of the most important parts of the body. Opening the wrist facilitates the smooth flow of Chi into the palm and fingers. In Zhan Zhuang this opening allows the Chi to freely exit, enter and re-circulate back into the organism. With Fa Jing applications, the wrist can be used to hold Chi and then suddenly release it. For proper release, the anterior part of the wrist must be fully elongated and especially the two central tendons leading into the palm.

As with the elbow, this region also contains powerful points that influence circulation and respiration. Located along the wrist crease, they are *Taiyuan* LU-9, *Daling* P-7 and *Shenmen* HT-7. In terms of Dim Mak application, these points are often struck first to set up the Chi disruption of the devastating points in the head, throat or torso.

In terms of health, *Taiyuan* is not only the Source Point of the Lung, it is also the Meeting Point for all the blood vessels in the body. Activating this point during practice increases the volume and ease of respiration and can help elongate and expand the blood vessels which facilitates the freer movement of Chi throughout the body.

A discussion of the wrist would not be complete without mentioning the lateral and medial regions, specifically the 'pukas' or indentations found there. These correspond to the areas around *Yangxi* LI-5 on the medial side and *Yanggu* SI-5 on the lateral side. The opening and elongating of these locations is invaluable when delivering a proper internal punch. You see, unlike the typical external punch where all the sinews contract, with an internal power punch, one elongates these regions at the moment of the whip or snap in order to completely release the power into the opponent.

**Hand**

The hand is the place where one's power and grace expresses itself. Once again, it is the opening of the wrist which makes issuing power through the hand, possible. This goes for both palm and fist. With the palm it is the elongation of the anterior portion of the wrist that transports the Chi into the all-important points of the palm, *Laogong* P-8 and *Shaofu* HT-8.

It is through these two points and the surrounding tissue that Chi exits the body and enters the opponent. In order to do this correctly, one must use the elongation in the palm and fingers to go from a slightly concave position (tile hand) to a convex position at the moment of release. In addition, there is a horizontal or lateral elongation component required in order to maintain sphericality. It is also through these two points that Chi can be transmitted for healing.

For punches, especially the traditional Tai Chi punch which is a vertical fist, we rely on the opening of *Yangxi* and *Yanggu* points to propel the Chi into the knuckles. With a linear, *Ji* sort of strike the elongation is equal. But in the *Peng* version where the fist arcs slightly upward at the end of the whip-like release, the elongation of the *Yanggu* region on the underside of the fist is necessarily more pronounced.

**Fingers**

Finally we come to the fingers. In Zhan Zhuang we want the fingers to gently lengthen without becoming stiff. We gain this by carefully opening each of the finger joints *without* locking them. Besides this vertical elongation, there is also a lateral or horizontal factor that must be taken into account. This stems mostly from the lateral opening of the palm and back of the hand. We notice it most in the space between the fingers. The fingers should feel lightly separated, as if there were little cotton balls between each of them.

The fingertips are important for many reasons, mainly sensitivity. This sensitivity can be developed all over the body and be used to feel an opponent's Chi and center upon contact. The fingertips can also emit incredibly focused Chi energy as in the 'Secret Sword' finger strike. At the other end of the spectrum, they can also be used to absorb external energy into the body for self-healing and rejuvenation or to emit stored Chi for healing another.

Now having gone through the body from top to bottom at least superficially, it's time to return our feeling-awareness to the Dan Tien. After this practice has been internalized, the above procedure can be accomplished in only a few minutes. For those less familiar, it is best to work with only one or two regions in detail during each session.

I have presented a fair amount of detailed information in this chapter. This approach parallels how the great pianist Franz Liszt approached learning music. Become familiar with *everything*. That way there will be nothing new or unfamiliar to be encountered that can move you off your center. This holds true for both martial arts and health. With martial arts, if we're familiar with every way a punch can be delivered, then we'll easily be able to recognize and adapt. With health, the more we know about our body and the Chi flow, the more we're able to control and direct the Chi effectively.

## STANDING DIFFERS FROM MOVING EXERCISE

Despite it's apparent simplicity, standing meditation is actually one of the most challenging things a person can do. One of the reasons is because Zhan Zhuang practice requires absolute mental, emotional and physical honesty. Let me explain. When we practice movement, whether it be Tai Chi, Xingyi or Bagua, especially at the beginning, it is easily possible to do it incorrectly and believe we're doing it right. Only later when the teacher corrects us, do we realize our error. This is where Zhan Zhuang is a little different.

Standing for an extended period of time, 40 minutes a day for health or 50 minutes to an hour or more for martial achievement, we cannot deceive ourselves into believing we're relaxed when we are not because sooner or later some uncomfortable sensation appears to remind us.

Therefore, when we finally do achieve some degree of relaxation, we can know it is genuine. Of course there are many, many deepening levels of relaxation that become available over the years.

An example of this can be a feeling of profound contentment, like we are exactly where we're supposed to be as a human being. Heaven above, the Earth below and we, man or woman in between, nothing to do, nothing to achieve, just pure beingness. Or sometimes we feel as if our muscles are 'melting.' When this occurs, the body will respond to our feeling-awareness and release blockages wherever we focus.

The same is true of *Nei Kung* 'energy experiences.' When we work with alchemical meditations or the like, our imagination becomes so refined that we can create experiences. But the question is, are these feelings and experiences real or just mock-ups of our imagination?

With Zhan Zhuang however, there is generally no question as to whether some energy or feeling is real. Since we are not seeking any particular experience, just greater relaxation, when something does happen, out-of-the-blue so to speak, we know it's real because we had no part in trying to create it. Also after one of these experiences, we are often able to duplicate and utilize the new awareness.

Of course the biggest difference between Zhan Zhuang and moving exercise is the direction of the experiential flow. With standing it is stillness that begets (internal) movement. But with moving exercise such as Tai Chi, we have exactly the opposite, in other words, out of movement we eventually find stillness.

If you think about it, Zhan Zhuang and Tai Chi compliment each other perfectly. Zhan Zhuang is the Yin energy that motivates action and Tai Chi is the Yang aspect which returns to stillness. In both methods there are many evolutionary cycles. With Zhan Zhuang we go from deeper levels of stillness to a more unified, whole-body movement. With Tai Chi, more unified whole-body movement invites a deeper and more profound sense of stillness.

A long time ago, the two methods were inseparable. Back in the day dedicated trainees often first began with sitting in a chair meditation. From there they stood up for an hour of Zhan Zhuang training. This was followed by walking exercises and repetition of individual form movements. Only then would they begin Tai Chi form practice, which would be done using multiple repetitions and in multiple manners. Slow, fast, large movements, small movements, with Jing to cultivate Yang Chi or with lightness and emptiness to nurture Yin Chi. There is an old saying, "...the Yang Chi is finite whereas the Yin Chi is infinite." Believe it or not, the above saying holds a big key to achievement at the higher levels.

## STRUCTURE VS. RELAXATION

When we begin Zhan Zhuang training, we very rapidly run into the apparent paradox of two seemingly opposing aspects - structure and relaxation. If, at the beginning we adhere too rigorously only to structure, we create counterproductive tension.

On the other hand, if we follow relaxation too exclusively, structure breaks down, greatly diminishing the benefits of the exercise. So, what to do? The answer lies in interchangeable use. And later in the unity of opposites.

Of course the idea is to assume a posture and then relax within it. But at the beginning, this is easier said than done. If in maintaining a posture, we generate too much tension (tight muscles) we can greatly restrict the flow of Chi. If this blockage continues past a certain point, problems can easily develop.

At the beginning it's hard to know the difference between 'good' tension and it's counterproductive step-brother, 'harmful' tension. In other words, when do we stand through the pain or discomfort, knowing that it is part of the healing process, and when do we utilize micro-movements to create relaxation and relief?

In the most traditional model, it's all trial-by-fire. We hold the posture regardless of any detrimental sensations such as pain, numbness, nausea etc., knowing that everything will eventually resolve itself.

While this is basically true, it could be months or even years until deep imbalances are resolved. In the mean time, we have to be prepared to endure a certain amount of discomfort as part of the healing process.

This is the original way, and if you're young and have a strong body with no injuries and a stoic personality, it can work for you. On the other hand, if you've had any serious injuries and/or are older, then the gentler way of relaxation will be preferred and here's why.

When I first began training, I asked the following question: What is more important, posture or relaxation? The answer I was given after long deliberation was *relaxation.*

While structure is obviously important for many reasons such as integration and Chi flow for example, it is the ability to relax more and more deeply that actually brings achievement.

Here it is important to point out that obsessive preoccupation with a posture's alignment will almost always bring negative results in the way of unwanted tension. Therefore, the symmetry of structure and the quest for its perfection can be deceiving, just look at nature. Nowhere in nature will we find symmetry in the way humans define it.

The branches of a tree are not symmetrical nor equidistant, or even completely straight for that matter and yet the tree thrives and grows healthy and tall. This means that the sooner we accept our imperfections and learn to be okay just the way we are, the faster our progress.

By concentrating on relaxation, eventually the body will begin to correct and adjust imbalances of itself, or 'suggest' to us how to work with the asymmetrical elements.

Here, there are two keys to remember.
1) The body's nature and motivation is always to heal itself.
2) The body has certain innate wisdoms we can trust.

That said, the best way to deal with this dilemma is a balanced approach, to use both elements, alignment (structure) and relaxation interchangeably.

The phrase, "Set it and forget it," is appropriate here. In other words, do your best to set up your structure and then let go of it and work mainly with relaxation.

So, we know that *only* relying on structure as the basis for our stand inevitably generates tension. This is what is meant when it is said, "You can practice for fifty years and gain nothing."

Now, in the strict martial arts tradition, you can soldier through the discomfort and pain and tough it out and eventually this tension will lessen and begin to resolve.

While this is fine for those seeking achievement in internal martial power, if we have injuries, this type of thinking could actually worsen the problem. But this is not to say that a certain amount of 'grit' isn't necessary for all practitioners no matter what their goal. For healing injuries however, this must be done very carefully and in moderation.

We will delve more deeply into the relationship between relaxation and the healing process later in this volume.

## BOTTOMS OF THE FEET ARE THE BENCHMARK

The feet are the place through which all the forces of gravity must pass. There are literally thousands of 'gravity filaments' or vertical lines of force throughout the body, all of which must be balanced and released from the top of the head and shoulders, down into the ground. In this way the front, back, insides and outsides of the bottoms of the feet, each reveal the result of our progressive relaxation.

The key here is evenness. Generally when we stand, especially at first, some parts of the feet will feel more pressure than others. By tracing these excesses (or deficiencies, not enough pressure) up their respective meridians, we can find the source of the resistance or blockage.

Once recognized, the next step is to relax and try to empty the suspect area and then continue to relax the relative muscle channel(s) all the way down under the bottom of the foot. Again, the goal here is *equal pressure*, no place too much or too little.

Finally, with enough practice even our feeling of this equal pressure inevitably disappears as we merge with the Earth. When this is accomplished we have effectively sunk the Chi and created, at least in part, the highly-prized state of *Sung*, sometimes spelled, *Song*.

So, wherever on the bottoms of the feet you feel uncomfortable, this is a reflection of tension elsewhere in the body. In other words, it indicates our body and/or our mind's inability to relax that line of gravity completely, throughout our entire structure.

On the other hand, the more we feel the pressure equalize throughout all parts of the foot, the more we feel these areas spread out, elongate and become even, the *better* our stand becomes. As this continues, we find the sensation of weight leaving the Central Channel, the center part of the body, and dwelling more in the Left and Right Channels.

This emptying is the beginning of the intermediate stages in the progression of the stand. From there, with continued practice the sensation of body weight in the left and right channels will also disappear as the Chi sinks under the bottoms of the feet and we discover the delicate balance of 'standing on the bones.'

At that point your root will be sunk deeply into the Earth, at which time you arrive at *Sung*, the relaxed interconnection of the skin, muscles, tendons, ligaments, bones, internal organs, glands, marrow and the *mind*. This includes both the *Xin*, heart-mind and *Yi*, intention.

Energetically we speak of the unification of the Chi. During the above mentioned process the Chi has become abundant, flooding the entire organism, leaving no place untouched.

And then there's the element of the different kinds of Chi within the body. For example, the *Ying* or nutritive Chi which travels with the blood. The *Wei Chi* or defensive energy. The Chi of the various internal organs, the *Zhang Fu*, and then there's the three external types of Chi, *Kong Chi*, air energy and breath. *Gu Chi*, literally translated as grain Chi from the food we eat and *Shui Chi* or water Chi from the liquids we drink. These three all interact with and effect the body's internal Chi processes as well.

**Unification of the Chi**

Now, since there are a number of different types of Chi, functioning throughout the body, how is it that the Chi can become unified? The answer to this is a little complex.

Basically, when we focus correctly within the low Dan Tien or navel area and do this repeatedly over a long period of time, we are able to bring more and more of our consciousness to bear, that is, more and more of our total beingness. This increase in the amount of consciousness we can focus eventually triggers a sort of chain reaction.

That is, it inevitably arouses and calls forth the all important pre-natal Chi from which all other types of the body's Chi are derived. Note that this pre-birth Chi is literally drawn from the *Ming Men*, where it is stored, into the low Dan Tien.

Under normal everyday conditions a portion of this pre-natal Chi would then enter the Kidney channels where it would ascend and be grasped by the Lungs and mixed with our breath. But when one is deep in Zhan Zhuang meditation in addition to that, something very different happens.

What seems to occur is, this pre-birth Chi or Essence, which comes from both parents and certain other karmic factors, becomes concentrated, nurtured, cultivated or *cooked*, and eventually transformed in the low Dan Tien, called by some the lower burning space. In this state it acts as both the fuel for the 'cooking fire,' as well as part of the 'food' to be cooked.

When this primal form of Chi becomes sufficiently abundant, it begins to overflow the bounds of the navel area and pour out, saturating the whole body. This extraordinary fullness of the pre-birth Chi then acts like a magnet which attracts all the other types of Chi. This is a bio-electromagnetic form of attraction. Like rivers returning to the sea. This relationship can be likened to the Sun and all the forms of life it supports.

The two factors that have triggered this reaction are:

1) The 'narrowness' and completeness of our focus.

2) The overwhelming magnetic quality of the pre-natal Chi.

It then follows that a certain amount of all the Chi in the body is drawn into the low Dan Tien.

Notice that I said a certain amount. This is an important distinction because if all the body's Chi were to actually sink to the low Dan Tien, or sink to the bottoms of our feet for that matter, we would certainly pass out and probably die due to the lack of function in the brain and internal organs.

So if only a percentage of the Chi needed to propagate and maintain the body's proper function actually gathers in the lower burning space, the question still remains, how does the Chi become 'unified?'

For the answer to this we must return to the image of the Sun and the relationship it has with all the growing things, plants, trees and the like, that it supports. What happens when the Sun appears each morning? All the plant's leaves for example, turn to greet it, to receive its life-giving nourishment.

So it is when the pre-birth Chi becomes sufficiently abundant in the low Dan Tien. All the other different types of Chi in the body, open their leaves so to speak.

This means they 'go into (magnetic) agreement' with the original creative pre-birth Chi and willingly align and blend their frequencies into the overall mix in the Dan Tien.

The result of all this is what's known as the unification of the body's Chi. But that's not quite the end of the matter.

When enough of this unified pre-birth and Ancestral Chi has been cultivated and transformed, this in turn begins to attract the original Heaven and Earth Chi from above and below and from whence it came.

It is at this point that a greater and greater unification takes place between the essence of our being and the beingness from which come the energies of Heaven and Earth. It is then that the highest levels of transformation become possible.

## THE FIVE POINTS OF THE FOOT

There are five locations on the bottoms of the feet, knowledge of which will greatly aid in our quest to open the body. They are:

1) *Yongquan* point - the Bubbling Well.

2) The center of the heel.

3) The Big Ball - located behind the big toe and the second toe.

4) The Little Ball - located behind the pinky toe and the 4th toe.

5) The Center Point, equidistant between the tip of the toes and the back of the heel. This point is located directly below *Jiexi* point ST-41. (see illustration)

There is a sixth point which also proves very useful. This is *Zulinqi* point, GB-41 and when properly relaxed and opened, has the power to help release the hip, especially the side of the hip. *Zulinqi* point is located on the top of the foot toward the outside, behind the 4th Metatarsophalangeal joint in a depression lateral to the tendon. (see illustration)

Each of the above points or regions can be seen and felt as having a correspondence to particular lines of gravity which descend through the body from the top of the head and the tops of the shoulders. Here is a very simplified version.

**Front**
Tissue toward the front of the body releases tension and body weight into the Bubbling Well and Centerpoint.

**Back**
Tissue toward the back of the body releases into the heel point.

**Outside**
Tissue toward the outsides of the body empties into *Zulinqi* point and the Little Ball.

**Inside**
Tissue toward the inside of the body (and leg) releases into the Big Ball, the Centerpoint and below the Medial Malleolus.

You can see by the description above, there are actually a number of shared or hidden correspondences for each of the basic four. As your practice deepens, many of these will become apparent. Also, when checking to see if the Chi has sunk, these locations assist in simplifying the task of isolating and resolving blockages, in other words having an idea where they come from.

For instance, a blockage in one's chest could show up as tension in the Big Ball, Centerpoint or even the Little Ball and *Zulinqi* point, depending on the actual location of the problem. A low back or lumbar injury would be reflected by tension or discomfort in or around the heel. Anyway, you get the idea.

Finally, it is important to note that focusing on the Bubbling Well will cause energy to *rise*, while focusing on the bottom of the heel will cause energy to *descend*.

Focusing on the Centerpoint will ideally allow energy to ascend and descend simultaneously. We automatically utilize these phenomena when we work with the more single-weighted postures.

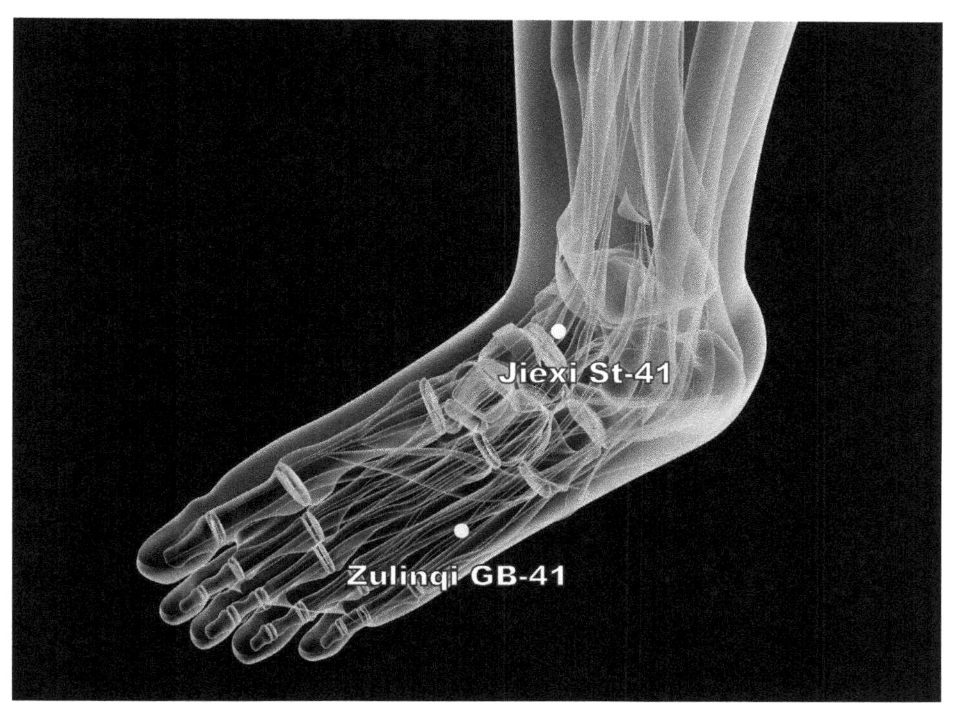


**Jiexi and Zulinqi Points**

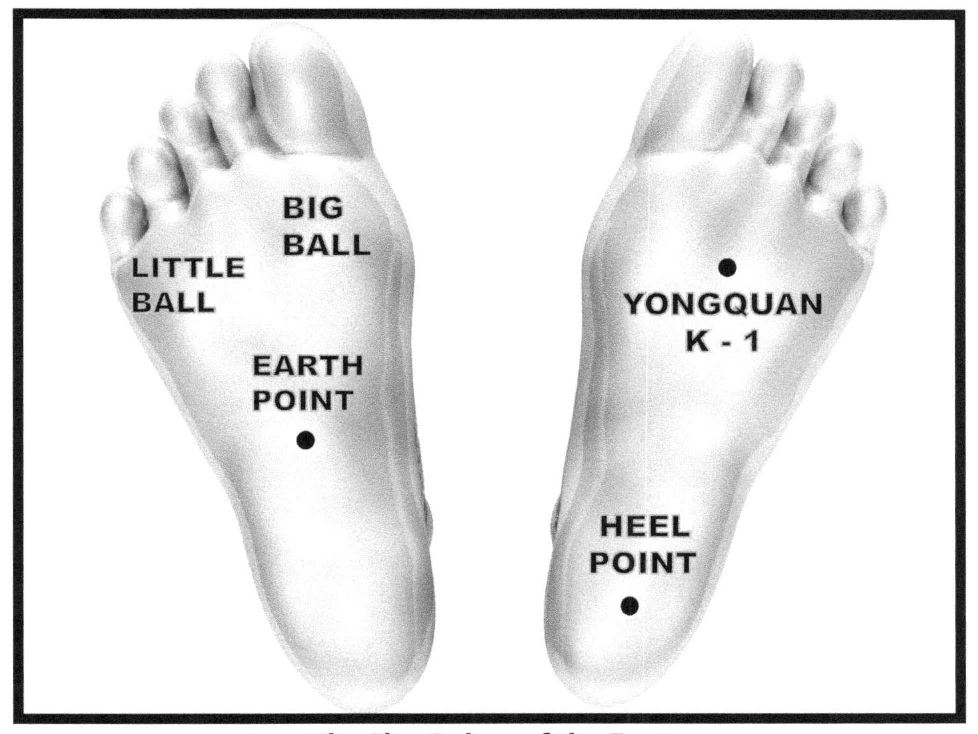


**The Five Points of the Foot**

# WORKING WITH STANDING POSTURES

# TWO APPROACHES TO RELAXATION

There are essentially two methods used to create relaxation as we enter into our stand. The first involves the *Yi*, intention and mental energy together with feeling while the second uses *Xin*, the heart-mind, with pure feeling and being exclusively.

**Method 1 - Using The Mind**
The first approach involves using the mind to square everything away, so to speak. That is, you go through the body step-by-step from the top of the head, down through the bottoms of the feet, correcting alignments, opening the various locations by relaxing and adjusting as necessary.

These adjustments can be anything from micro-movements to pure *Nei Kung*, using the mind to influence the body. We'll talk more about this aspect later. This first method is helpful when we have difficulty quieting the mind.

Concentrating in this manner gives the mind something to do and tends to get rid of excessive thought. Once we have gone through the whole body, we then find our center and automatically shift to the second method.

**Method 2 - Using Pure Feeling**
The second method is deceptively simple. "Don't think, feel!" This Bruce Lee aphorism uttered in the movie Enter the Dragon, says it all.

In other words, briefly use the mind to put your body in the most balanced posture possible at that moment, find your center and then forget the mind and enter the realm of pure feeling and being.

This second approach is actually both the beginning and the end of practice. By this I mean, at the outset of our training we use this method in order to begin to feel what is actually going on and learn the true state of our body. After many years of daily practice, one still uses this method because the single-pointed focus of their feeling-awareness is all that is needed to motivate the Chi.

With both methods the goal is the same; calm the mind and settle the emotions in order to relax the body. All three factors, physical emotional and mental are *both* interconnected and reciprocal. So, the success we have in calming the mind is reflected by a release of tension in the body.

The same is true of settling the emotions. The difference here is that in addition to effecting the body in general, settling the emotions effects each of our internal organs. This can have a profound effect not only in calming the body, but also balancing our overall state of being. To put it another way, by their very nature, certain strong emotions like anger, frustration, impatience, deep sadness or fear, agitate the mind. Creating excess thinking automatically generates tension in the body. The same is true when the mind obsessively dwells on problems. Repetitive negative thoughts or mental loops, trigger one or more of the above listed emotions which results in concomitant tensions in the body.

If you find yourself in this position during your stand, it has been my experience that doing one or more of the Six Healing Sounds Chi Kung can help ameliorate the imbalance. This method is easily searchable on YouTube. But know this, what's usually presented is only the basic components. There are a number of *Nei Kung* add-ons such as the use of color and the direction from which the color enters the body and particular organ for example, which can *greatly enhance* the results.

## FINDING YOUR CENTER

There are a number of ways to find one's center. The following method has been found to work extremely well.

1) Place the top of one hand on your navel or Dan Tien area and the top of the back of the other hand at the acupuncture *Ming Men* just below the second lumbar vertebra on the low back. If you like you can spread out the fingers of the back hand in order to feel the Chi Kung *Ming Men*, just above the Sacrum, as well. With a judicious hand placement you can cover both.

2) Once your hands are in position, move your feeling awareness from your front hand, through the body to your back hand.

3) Then move your feeling from your back hand to a point inside your body, halfway between back and front.

4) Lastly, lower your hands to your sides (Wuji posture) and just feel.

For those who prefer more specificity, five locations can be used.

**Five Regions - Front to Back**
1) The outside of the abdomen, the skin where your hand is touching.
2) The low Dan Tien, 2 to 4 inches inside the body.
3) The Centerpoint, equidistant between front and back.
4) Inside of the Lumbar vertebra, 2 to 4 inches in from the back.
5) The outside of the back, where your other hand is touching.

At first your centerpoint location may be vague or amorphous, but with continued practice, it will become refined to a single point. After that, many wonderful things begin to happen, such as the spontaneous opening of various channels, energy centers or even the entire energy body itself.

Remember to find your center by going from *back to front*, not the other way around.

The reason for this is that we as human beings have much more awareness of the front of our bodies than we do of our backs. Without going from the back first, there is a tendency to skew our awareness of the centerpoint.

And finally there's the matter of our 'Center' itself. Just exactly what is it? We will understand the answer best if we first examine what it is not.

The tissues and organs in the physical region of the Dan Tien are the Intestines and Bladder as well as all the surrounding muscles. It is clearly apparent that this Center of ours is not actually part of any of these physical substrates otherwise science would have discovered and in some way measured it. That's what scientists do.

So, if our Center is not actually physical, then what is it? And how if it's not physical, can it possibly effect the human body? Our Center is actually part of our etheric or electromagnetic body and some other subtle bodies present within the human organism.

That being the case, it is not the physical senses that can recognize, feel and work with the energy of the Center. Rather, it is a different set of senses, similar to the physical ones, but much more highly refined.

It is said in the meditative practices that the warmth we feel in the Dan Tien is a sign of the Chi, not actually the Chi itself.

To access the realm of Chi, one must be able to calm the mind and emotions and slip into a state of partial emptiness. It is from this apparent emptiness that the subtle senses awaken and become available to us.

So, how does this powerful but subtle Chi energy influence our bodies? The answer lies in the theory of 'Returning to the Origin,' meaning, the physical is created from non-physical energy which in turn finds its origin in an even more subtle energy field and so forth, all the way back to the source of all energy. It is this inter-connective commonality that actually facilitates and expedites the Chi's role and influence.

## ADJUSTING POSTURES

When we see pictures of *Yiquan* postures, most of the time we find the arms appear quite extended. By extension I am referring to the distance of the elbows from the spine and also the distance of the hands from the chest. These postures seem to stretch the body to its limit and even beyond.

This is all well and good if your body is already open, but if not, there are many times painfully strong repercussions. Hence the reputation for Zhan Zhuang's difficulty.

First, it must be said that if you use the traditional extended-arms method, all the benefits which I'm about to describe will *probably* accrue *eventually*, but the road will be long and hard and as a result, filled with many elements of confusion and discomfort.

Nevertheless, if you put in the daily and yearly requisite practice time, much will become clear and eventually some order will emerge from the chaos. This is the traditional model which is fine if you start training in your twenties or thirties. Unfortunately this trial-by-fire method is not suitable for many people, especially those in their later years.

So, what to do? Having first been taught in the traditional manner myself, after a time I was forced to make certain modifications, due to injuries I'd suffered.

I shall endeavor now to illustrate the efficacy of a modified approach called the Circumscribed Method and the many benefits that accumulate as a result. But before we can start standing in this way, we must make some minor adjustments to the arms and shoulder-girdle.

## Adjusting Posture Technique

(See photo sequence) In the first photo we see the traditional position, slightly exaggerated to show the pressure on the spine, back and neck.

The second photo in the sequence shows the withdrawal of the elbows and forearms back toward the spine. When this has been accomplished, there should be very little if any 'pulling pressure' in the upper back muscles.

Photo three. Now, here's where it can get a little tricky. The next stage is to condense (stretch inwardly) all the tissue from the finger tips back into the attachments of the spine. And when we do this progressively, we must do so along the lines of the bones with only a minimal reduction or alteration in the posture.

For this to happen, we will follow all the vectors of the posture's bone structure. This is really closing and opening the joints while stretching (and later spiraling) the tissue into and out of our centerline.

The fourth photo portrays the result of releasing and opening the tissue we've just condensed, back out from the spine to the finger tips. The various releases necessary to do this will be discussed in detail later. For now, here's the rundown from the finger tips back into the spine.

1) Telescope the fingers into the palm and back of hand, creating a 'Tile hand.' The hand has a slight 'V' shape, like a Chinese roof tile.

2) Condense the palm and back of the hand into the wrist.

3) Close the wrist joint and at the same time, stretch and condense all the tissue of the forearm, back into the elbow joint.

4) Close the elbow joint and condense all the tissue of the upper arm, back and up into the shoulder.

5) Close the shoulder joint. This involves mostly the deltoids and may cause the elbow to withdraw very slightly back and in.

6) Now, using the Teres muscles at the back of the shoulders, stretch the shoulders slightly back and in toward the shoulder blades.

7) Finally, using the Rhomboids, condense (lightly pull) the shoulder blades toward the spine.

In terms of the joints we can think of telescoping, that is, a retracting compression. In terms of the muscles, we talk of condensing or stretching backwards or inwards. Closing from the extremities into our center or centerline and then opening, expanding and stretching back out from the spine to the finger tips.

These techniques can be done either in a completely linear manner or later with a spiral condensing, but always without breaking postural alignments.

**1 - Traditional Extension**

**2 - Withdrawing Elbows**

**3 - Condensing Tissues**

**4 - Releasing and Opening Tissues**

## THE CIRCUMSCRIBED METHOD

Two of the main goals in Zhan Zhuang training are integration and unity. The Circumscribed Method allows us to engage and integrate the greatest amount of tissue from the start, while at the same time, bringing to our conscious awareness the locations that are not cooperating due to blockage.

The idea is easy. Rather than disengaging certain muscles, instead of integrating them when we try to duplicate a teacher's posture, and force advanced alignments on the body, we start by setting as our limitation, the body's *weakest link.*

Simply put, this means if, let's say we're working with the upper back, shoulders and arms, and we have a tight muscle around there, we become aware of it's more limited range of motion and avoid any change in postural alignment that would force the suspect area beyond what it can properly do at the time of practice. This means to use only a *relaxed* stretch.

The incorrect opening of the muscles and sinews is largely responsible for much of the discomfort of arbitrarily assumed postures.

In fact, in the shoulder area, this exaggeration will cause in the novice, all or part of their shoulders and/or upper-back to become raised instead of relaxed downward and apart. This lifting of the shoulder muscles and other muscle groups is a real no-no in that it destroys both integration and root.

In this example we'll work with the basic 'Holding the Ball,' or 'Embracing The Tree' posture. Normally when you assume this posture, the tips of the elbows are placed in front of the plane of the chest and abdomen, often quite far in front so that the arms are very extended.

Again, let me repeat, this posture is fine as long as there are no violations as you open into it. This means that all the muscles in the shoulders and upper back must be *continually dropped out and elongated* downward as you extend your arms to maximum distance. If, for even an instant, that feeling of downward relaxation is disrupted or stopped, it's all over, because you've just hyper-extended and broken your alignments. There's only one thing to do, start again! But now we'll employ the Circumscribed Method to insure that this doesn't happen.

1) Instead of setting the tips of your elbows far beyond the plane of the chest as in the traditional manner, pull them back toward the spine until they're roughly at the midline of the sides of your body.

That puts your hands and forearms much closer to the chest and this is where we begin to create an alignment that engages all the muscles, leaving nothing out.

2) Next, as you exhale, and without raising your shoulders one iota, gently lift up your elbows, forearms and hands as one unit about an inch or so, then condense all your joints and tissues back into the spine, working with each segment as described earlier.

3) Now inhale, relax and release the tops of the shoulders, the shoulder blades, chest and the upper back downward as far as you can. As this is occurring, relax your arms so the elbows descend to where they were and you feel both a dropping down and forward 'rounding' feeling coming from each side of the spine.

4) If you were successful, in addition to the elbows wanting to drop under and move forward of themselves, you should also feel a lateral expansion. The tips of the elbows will want to move further from the sides of the torso, as well as under and forward.

When letting go of the back muscles, start from the centerline and spine near *Dazhui* point. Release outward to the sides as you release downward to the bottom of the shoulder blades. What we're looking for is the feeling that the torso and arms, connect or unify.

The idea is to feel as if the upper, and eventually even the lower back muscles, are being gently stretched and rounded like a barrel. Another sign that you have done this correctly, is that your arms seem to be somewhat weightless.

They can even feel like they're floating. One of the reasons for this is muscular integration, meaning the large muscles of the back are sharing in the task of keeping the arms aloft.

Another reason is an increased Chi flow moving through your newly acquired integrated linkage. With enough practice everything (dropping out both vertically and horizontally as well as lowering the elbows and rounding the arms) happens simultaneously.

And it is from this idea of simultaneous movement on two planes that both spiral and spherical energies are derived.

At first, these movements should be fairly pronounced in order to feel each part of the linkage adjust and move into place. The fact is though, once refined, these openings and closings, stretchings and condensings, become essentially micro-movements and therefore many times, not easily visible. The first photo below shows the traditional long stretch

where the elbows are at such a distance from the spine that they often create too much pressure in the thoracic and cervical vertebrae.
The second photo shows the result of the Circumscribed Method after first applying the Adjusting Posture technique. Notice the downward or rounded feeling in the back, shoulders and elbows with the Circumscribed Method, whereas with the traditional extended method there is a far greater intimation of *Ji* or forward projecting energy. Here I speak of *Ji* as part of the four basic internal energies, *Peng, Lu, Ji* and *An*. Not to be confused with the Tai Chi postures of the same names.

**Adjusting Posture Technique - Expansion Sequence**
1) Relax the tissue around *Dazhui* and the spine. Release the Rhomboids downwards as you stretch them toward the shoulder blades.

2) Gently drop the shoulder blades and chest, and stretch the Teres muscles down and out from the shoulder blades toward the upper arm.

3) Release and open the shoulder joint and relax the upper arm muscles downward. This will cause the elbow to drop slightly down and forward.

4) Open the elbow joint.

5) Stretch the tissue of the forearm down into the wrist.

6) Open the wrist joint and elongate the palm and back of the hand.

7) Elongate the fingers by opening each of the finger joints.

Please note: the Circumscribed Method and Adjusting Postures Technique can be applied to any arm posture with great efficacy.

**Traditional Opening**

**Circumscribed Opening**

## UNIFYING THE BODY

In the final analysis the major goal of our Zhan Zhuang training is 'Unity.' This unity we speak of is both the journey and the goal and for this to take place, many changes will have had to occur in the physical and subtle bodies. One of the first steps in achieving this overall unity is the integration of body, mind, emotions and spirit.

Unification of the body begins at the most basic level with our alignments, specifically the positioning of our bone structure.

The next phase is the integration of the muscles, fascia and sinews. It is here that we generally encounter the cellular memory of previous events that have affected the body. It is also in this phase that one experiences the discomforts or pains of old injuries as they surface to be resolved.

Once some of these old problem areas heal and open up, we begin to feel the difference between individual muscles *disappear*, and in its place we feel a 'totality' of particular regions in the body. After much training this feeling of totality encompasses the entire structure and eventually the entire human organism.

In order to accomplish the above, we will have had to delve far beyond the muscle and bone structure into the internal organs and the emotions stored in each, and then fathom the glands, marrow and brain.

When one accesses the level of the bone marrow in Zhan Zhuang, elements of Marrow Washing can occur spontaneously. Of course, this goes a long way to actually rejuvenating the body and leading it back into radiant health.

As part of this extended course of training, one must learn to link each part of the body to a central source. In the case of the physical body this location is the low Dan Tien, our physical power center. This process of linking is often called 'hardwiring,' and will be discussed in a later section.

No discussion about unifying the body would be complete without addressing the role of the breath.

In the old way of internal martial arts training, breathing patterns were not usually introduced until the student had mastered all the dynamics of both individual postures and movements and in the case of Tai Chi, even the form itself. Until that time, the student was simply advised to 'breathe naturally' and not hold their breath. And there is a hidden wisdom in this.

What they found was that once a person had mastered all the basics and could do these things right, the correct breathing would arise of itself. These intuitive breathing patterns can take the form of either the natural breath (inhale-expand, exhale-condense) or the reverse breath. (inhale-condense, exhale-expand) Or an interplay or exchange between the two.

After a time, especially in Zhan Zhuang, this natural pattern will begin to emulate the cycle of the Universal Pulse and develop into whole-body or spherical breathing.

By definition, once you start making a conscious decision about when to inhale and when to exhale, you have *Chi Kung*. But with *Nei Kung*, the breathing element is generally ignored in favor of the single-pointed focus of our feeling-awareness. How can you have single-pointed focus if a part of you is thinking about the breath?

In Tai Chi, this problem is solved by hardwiring the breathing cycles to the movements and with enough practice this becomes automatic. In other words you don't have to think about it. Once this occurs, we're ready for the *Nei Kung* practices. With Zhan Zhuang, it is through stillness that the *Nei Kung* strategies manifest. It is then that we begin to understand the various energetic combinations and integrations of the diverse types of Chi present, both inside the body and without. This leads to an understanding of the merging and unification of the Chi through the various alchemical processes that occur in standing meditation.

Here is a list of the elements involved in the unification of the body.

1) Muscles, Tendons, Ligaments and Bones

2) Nervous System - the link between physical and energetic systems.

3) Internal Organs - contain both physical and energetic components.

4) Glands

5) Bone Marrow

6) Brain

The aspect of the breath can not only assist in the overall unification process, but also serve as a benchmark by which we can judge our progress. You see, as more and more of the above elements lock into place, the breath will seem to progressively fill more and more of the body. The goal is to breathe like a baby, that is, the breath oxygenates every cell in the body. And once again we have whole-body or spherical breathing.

## THE IMPORTANCE OF HARDWIRING

In *Yiquan* and Zhan Zhuang as with all the internal martial arts, there are many embedded layers of deeper and deeper integration, body coordination and application. On the physical side this includes, bone alignments, opening and closing the joints, stretching the tissue linearly and spiraling the tissue. On the *Nei Kung* side, there are also many phases such as working with the Left and Right *Chi Kung* Channels, working with the Central Channel, working with the organs and glands, etc.

Hardwiring is the mechanism that enables the linkage of the many parts of the body to a central location, in this case, the low Dan Tien. Later, in advanced practices, this central focus can be in other areas like the middle and upper Dan Tien or even multiple regions. But for health and indeed martial power, for now we'll focus exclusively on the low Dan Tien or navel area. This method is most suitable to Zhan Zhuang as well as the other internal arts.

Judicious use of hardwiring allows us to actualize the embedded layers of coordination available in each posture or movement. On a physical level, what we do is focus on one particular part of the body at a time in relationship to a central point, in order to create what some have called a dimmer switch.

That is, the ability to activate part or all of one's unified energy at will by focusing on just one energy center. For now, two basic examples should suffice to clarify the technique. The first method uses breathing to create the linkage, while the second relies on repetitive movement.

The Breathing Method: Choose a part of the body. In the beginning this should probably be somewhere in the torso. For this example we'll use the upper back. Next, focus your breathing in the low Dan Tien for a few rounds, until you feel a relative evenness between the inhale and the exhale. A feeling of body relaxation begins to occur. During this process you will have sensed a gentle expansion and condensing in the lower abdominal area. Now quietly shift your attention to your upper back and feel it expand and condense with the abdomen. Continue this process for a number of rounds while periodically shifting your feeling-awareness back and forth between the two areas.

With continued practice you will almost be able to be aware of the two locations simultaneously. I say almost because our brain has the ability to switch between the two places at lightening speed, such that it almost feels simultaneous.

I'm speaking about our conscious awareness here. First we feel this, then we feel that, only really really fast.

However, there is another method which can superimpose or join the two locations completely. For that we must access our peripheral feeling-awareness while basically letting go of our fixed conscious focus and allowing it to become more amorphous.

Here's how: Focus your conscious feeling-awareness in your physical center which falls on the plane of the navel area, specifically, halfway between the navel and the outside of the back. Now, while keeping some of your conscious feeling-awareness there, let your peripheral feeling-awareness open to the region of the upper back. Feel the two locations rise and fall in unison.

Later, in the *Nei Kung* practices you can create a sphere in your center and feel it expand and condense, taking whatever part(s) of the body you desire to link with it. Later, these spheres will begin to rotate, similar to the Dan Tien Rotation famous in Chen Tai Chi style. This turning or spinning is important because of how it amplifies, propels and accelerates the Chi.

Eventually hardwiring will include the entire body, from head to toe and from inside to outside. When accomplished, our center will now act much like a dimmer switch in its ability to power the body's overall energetic state either up or down, that is, increase or decrease it at will.

In order to continue the hardwiring procedure, repeat the earlier basic process to link each region to the center, one-at-a-time. Please note, this should first start with the exterior muscles and sinews and then proceed inward to the deeper parts of the body, organs etc.

Now for the Moving Method. This technique uses all the principals of the previous method, only now we apply the same foci while moving, say in Tai Chi form movements for example.

So, while doing each movement singly and repeatedly, we look at one part of the body in relation to what the center is doing. Let's choose the knees. What are our knees doing in relationship to the low Dan Tien during a particular movement? Are they coordinated, retaining their alignment, expanding and condensing in unison, sending and receiving, opening and closing together as one?

The progression of hardwiring begins with individual areas of the body being linked to the center, but from there it expands step-by-step to include more locations simultaneously until eventually 'everything' is linked in.

A good way to proceed after attaining the basic individual mastery is to use the external six harmonies. This involves hardwiring certain parts of the body to each other in addition to the Dan Tien. For example, we can work the linkage between the elbows and knees and then later use multiple pairs such as the shoulders and hips *and* elbows and knees.

In Zhan Zhuang, the easiest way to affect linkage both to the Dan Tien as well as from one part to another, is by using the breath. With the Dan Tien method, breathe into the low Dan Tien and abdominal region until you begin to feel a gently rounded sensation like a sphere getting larger on the inhale and smaller during the exhale. Next, while keeping a percentage of your feeling-awareness in your abdomen, divert the rest of your feeling-awareness to the region you wish to hardwire. Relax the region as you inhale and expand the abdomen, allowing it to open and condense in unison with the Dan Tien.

As you continue cycling your breath, you can check on both locations by rapidly moving your feeling-awareness between the two. When you get it right, you will find that the rhythmic expansion and contraction of the two locations and the breath, will have activated the Universal Pulse. This is the breathing of the Earth and the world around us including the sun, moon, planets and stars.

Once this is in place all the body's tissue will be moving in concert as the Chi circulates, uninhibited. At that point you're well on your way to achieving what the Classics call 'stillness in motion.'

Eventually, while the majority of your conscious feeling-awareness is held in your center, your peripheral feeling-awareness allows you to simultaneously feel what the rest of the body is doing. Hopefully this will be pulsing or moving like one big, single-celled unit.

## WORKING WITH THE BREATH

One eventual goal of our standing meditation is Whole Body Breathing. Although, once this is achieved, that is, hardwired and happening on it's own, the sense of breath will seem to go away as our super-refined focus becomes fully absorbed in feeling the Chi, both inside the body and out.

Here is a good method to begin unifying the breath. Start by breathing into the upper back and lower belly (Dan Tien area) simultaneously. As you continue to relax, you will notice the breath in the upper back will seem to fill more and more downward while the breath in the lower belly seems to expand upward.

Once the breath naturally reaches the Clavicle in the upper front and the Sacrum in the lower back, more advanced methods can be used.

One of the most important steps on the way to Whole Body or Spherical Breathing is what might be called 'Separation Breathing.' This is the ability to have various muscle groups move in different directions while we breathe.

Specifically, I'm talking about the Rectus Abdominis and the Obliques, more exactly the ability to differentiate between the Internal and External Obliques. But I'm getting ahead of myself. Before we can move the tissues in multiple directions we must first master moving everything in one direction at a time.

What happens when one normally exhales is that the abdomen withdraws somewhat toward the spine and slightly upward. What we want to do is gently accentuate this natural motion. So, as you exhale, withdraw the abdomen inward and then lift slightly upwards under the ribs. This must be from the Pubic bone up through the diaphragm. Then as you inhale, relax and release the same muscles downward and *fill from the bottom up*. The axiom is: 'In and up, down and out.' Once you can do this, we need to add the rest of the torso to the process.

Now, while exhaling also withdraw and lift the chest muscles, Pectoralis Major and Minor, up under the clavicle. Here it is important to point out the term 'inward' also refers to lateral movement, from the sides to the center in addition to the vertical movement. Naturally this applies to the lower abdomen as well.

With this now under our belts, it's time to work with the back by itself first and then in unison with the front. The back muscles work in essentially the same manner as the front.

Upon exhaling we very gently draw the back muscles up and in from right above the Sacrum to just below the top of the shoulders and toward *Dazhui*, the Big Vertebrae. While doing this, we must never raise the shoulders.

From there, we begin the inhale by releasing the tissues we've lifted and filling again from the bottom up. From the low back, up through the shoulders.

When finally the above methods become natural, that is, they happen almost automatically during the stand, we are ready to tackle Separation Breathing aka, Tai Chi breathing.

This is the technique that eventually becomes Spherical or Whole Body Breathing. This method incorporates all the previous techniques (combined front and back methods) as well as the ability to separate and control the External and Internal Obliques.

Let me explain. As we exhale, softly drawing all the tissue up and in, we use gravity to gently compress the midriff. (the space between the top of the hip to the low ribs on the side) Then upon inhaling, in addition to releasing the tissue and filling from the bottom up, we must also lift the Internal Obliques to expand the space in the midriff we just compressed. Please note that this lift is mostly a product of the breath (the inhale) rather than a physical lifting.

Only lift the Internal Obliques, all the other tissue, the Rectus Abdominis, External Obliques, the Pectoralis Major and Minor and all the back muscles are dropping down, hence the term Separation. When this is done correctly we clearly feel both downward and upward movement at the same time. Later, we will expand to also include the legs and arms.

Lastly I need to explain something further about releasing the tissue and filling from the bottom on the inhale. This is the final piece of the puzzle necessary to create the multi-directional movement seamlessly.

The key is this. As we inhale, rather than releasing all the lifted muscles at one time, instead, we relax downward and fill from the bottom, up, in the following sequence. First release the tissue from the navel to the Pubic bone, then inhale, expand and fill from the Pubic bone, back up to the navel. Use the same procedure from the Solar Plexus to the navel and finally from the Clavicle to the Solar Plexus.

Now release (drop out) and breathe into each section of the back. From the *Ming Men* to the Sacrum, from the low ribs to the *Ming Men*, from right below the tips of the Shoulder Blades to the low ribs and lastly from *Dazhui* to below the Shoulder Blades. Once this has been achieved, we must then do both front and back at the same time.

I have used these large areas as the example (this is the preliminary method) but later all this must be done inch by inch, from the bottom up. When this becomes smooth, we actually feel in our bodies what the Classics say, "...in order to move upward, first move downward" or "go down to go up."

Each of these methods can be said to evolve naturally using the one pointed-focus. But on its own, this often takes many years to occur. The above techniques, if used carefully, allow us to achieve at least a basic form of unification far more rapidly.

Please note, these techniques must be approached very gently, otherwise you risk stagnating the Chi, which believe me, you don't want to do. The fact is, working with anything other than one's natural breath, has at least the potential to create problems. Having a knowledgeable teacher who can supervise this can be most useful. This is also why much of the above material was only taught orally, one on one.

But since a proper instructor might not be available, I will briefly list some of the warning signs.

The main sign is some sort of pain, tightness or discomfort. Also dizziness or nausea. If this occurs, discontinue your session and simply breathe normally (your natural breath) while walking around or go sit or lay down and relax.

The thing is, and this is where it gets tricky. Certain types of odd feelings, discomfort and even some kinds of pain can be considered part of the normal process of the body opening up and healing. Distinguishing between the types of sensations is where a knowledgeable teacher becomes invaluable.

# WUJI POSTURE: THE QUICKEST WAY TO THE SPINE

## WUJI: THE QUICKEST WAY TO THE SPINE

In terms of the awareness of our spine, the Wuji posture has a great advantage when compared to any of the arms-raised postures. That advantage is the simple fact that our arms remain at our sides. By leaving our arms relaxed in this manner, our attention more naturally stays inside the torso. But don't take my word for it, test this for yourself.

First, stand with your hands at your sides for a minute or so. Then raise your arms and form the 'Holding the Ball' posture or any other arms-raised position you choose and maintain that for a minute.

Notice that as soon as you raise your hands, your conscious attention naturally tends to shift away from the torso as a whole, to the arms and upper body. Finally, return your arms to the sides of the body and notice what happens. Your feeling-awareness begins to leave the arms and return to the torso.

It is the Wuji posture's natural focus within the torso that allows our feeling-awareness to more easily become conscious of the spine and the tissue attached to it.

In addition to the arm position in the Wuji posture, there is another factor that can also influence our spinal awareness. And that is the width of the feet. When we use stances that are wider than hip width, like the shoulder width stance for example, then just as with the arms, our feeling attention tends to move to the outsides of the body.

It is important to note here that if one stands with feet wider than shoulder width, there is no longer any actual 'rooting,' but rather something called 'Bracing.' Bracing develops very strong legs, but it doesn't develop *root*. These wider *Ma* or horse-stances are used in Japanese Karate as well as in a number of Kung Fu styles.

On the other hand, when we position the feet at hip width, the alignment of our bones allows for greater muscular relaxation. This allows our perception to better penetrate the spine.

This is even more true, when at an advanced level, we reduce the distance between our feet to narrower than hip width. Of course for this to work, we must stretch the body vertically to compensate for the reduction in width.

Oddly enough, this additional vertical stretch not only develops root, but also brings greater awareness of the spine. And since all the nerves from the internal organs connect along the spinal column, greater awareness of this area is invaluable.

Also, the various hand positions used with the Wuji posture can go a long way to healing and deeper cultivation. In the next section, I will provide further insight into the role and use of the arms and hands in the Wuji posture.

## THE NATURAL POSITION

There are a number of hanging arm and hand positions that can be used for differing effects with the Wuji posture. They are the Natural position, the Taoist position, the Shoulder-Stretch position, the Beaks position and the Closed-Fist position.

We will begin with the Natural position. This is the most basic. The arms and hands simply hang freely, although there are almost as many individual variations as there are practitioners.

Those with tight shoulders and neck will find their arms touching or almost touching their bodies. For those who are more advanced, the armpits will be open and the arms and hands will hang some distance from the sides of the body and a little in front.

It's generally a good idea at any level, to do a couple of shoulder shrugs to fully release any tension in the shoulder tops before settling into your posture. Simply lift your shoulders up an inch or two and then suddenly drop them, like cutting the strings of a marionette. Let them fall and dangle where they will. You can do this several times if you like. Afterward, the idea is to surrender the neck, shoulders and arms to gravity. By this I mean, allow the downward force of gravity to elongate each of the joints, including those of the fingers.

Often it will be the case that one's fingers will be unable to naturally elongate, in fact they can be quite curled up. There are a number of reasons for this. Usually, if the problem's not severe arthritis of the hand, you'll find the difficulty stemming from further up the chain, meaning the neck, shoulders, elbows or wrist. Often as you resolve issues there, you'll find your fingers naturally elongating by themselves.

**Wuji Posture - Natural Position**

## THE TAOIST POSITION

The second position, and one of my personal favorites, is the Taoist position which places the side of the hand at *Hegu* point LI-4, touching near *Fengshi* point GB-31 on the leg. *Fengshi* point is about halfway between the hip joint and the knee joint, roughly along the centerline of the side of the leg and a little behind it.

One of the reasons I use this posture a great deal is because of it's ability to help create an overall body balance.

By placing the sides of the hands along the centerline of the sides of the thighs, muscles that need to drop down the front of the body tend to do so and those that should drop down the back, do likewise.

To get a picture of this, imagine a plane that bisects the tops of the shoulders, all the way down through the torso and legs. All tissues in front of the plane, release down the front half of the body, while all the tissues behind the plane, release down the back half.

This division actually applies from the top of the head all the way down to the bottoms of the feet and is only one of the many Yin-Yang correspondences available in Zhan Zhuang.

By creating this balanced front and back effect, not only do we balance our postural alignments, but we also facilitate a more balanced flow of Chi throughout the body, including to the organs and brain.

There is one variation of this posture which is also used. Instead of resting the side of the hand on the thigh, we turn the palm to face the leg and touch *Fengshi* point with the tip of the long finger. This has the effect of recycling the Chi, back into the body.

**Wuji Posture - Taoist Position**

## SHOULDER-STRETCH POSITION

The Shoulder-Stretch position is excellent for those just starting out or with neck or shoulder problems. This posture places the backs of the wrists in the depressions at the height of the hip bone (Posterior Iliac Crest) toward the outsides of the back.

Standing with the arms and hands in this manner causes the muscles of the upper back and shoulders, specifically the Trapezius, Rhomboids, Teres and Deltoids to be stretched downward and outward, away from the spine.

This in turn will create more space in those regions and facilitate a better Chi flow. Be careful however that the specific placement of the hands doesn't cause the tops of your shoulders to rise or lift.

A good way to test this method is to first place the arms and hands in the Natural, or Taoist position and stand for a little while. After a couple of minutes switch to the Shoulder-Stretch position and hold that for a little while, and then return to your original posture. You will soon find that things feel different, more relaxed and open.

It is important with the Shoulder-Stretch position to keep the chest and shoulder blades relaxing downward as there will be a tendency for some to stick out their chest or raise their shoulder blades due to the demands of the posture itself. This is especially true for those with any tightness or injuries in the upper back, neck or shoulders.

Later, as one becomes thoroughly comfortable with this method, all the tissue on either side of the spine will begin to gently stretch outward. This lateral expansion will then percolate down the back and into the hips, legs and feet.

**Wuji Posture - Shoulder-Stretch Position**

## THE BEAKS POSITION

A more sophisticated variation of the Shoulder-Stretch method is the Beaks position. The beak I'm referring to is the same Beak used in Tai Chi's Single Whip.

Start with your arms hanging at your sides. Form beaks with both hands, then point the fingers backwards, behind you. From there simply rotate the beaks outward, away from the body.

That's really all there is to it, but the key to success lies in how you form the beaks. The beaks must be created by first elongating the wrist, the back of the hand and the fingers.

Next, while still elongating, touch all the fingers to some part of the thumb. This is like activating a circuit. Be sure to not bend the finger joints any more than is absolutely necessary while doing this.

Now, while still keeping the extension in your wrists, the backs of your hands and your fingers, open your upper back and shoulders and twist the wrists outward, until the finger tips face away from the thighs. Your forearms should be roughly on a line with the back of the hips.

In terms of stretch, the Beaks position is like the Shoulder-Stretch method on steroids. In addition to the powerful stretch it generates, the Beaks position tends to keep the energy recycling within the organism although it's also possible to use the tips of the fingers and thumb and the space between them, to vent excess energy. It should be noted here that rather than bending the finger joints too much, it's okay to keep a small gap between the fingers and thumb. This type of slightly open beak was used in ancient times as a way to deliver Chi and energize an acupuncture needle.

**Wuji Posture - Beaks Position**

## THE CLOSED-FIST POSITION

The Closed-Fist position is in essence for healing and conserving energy. It uses elements of both the Taoist and Beaks positions.

In this method, we begin with the arms hanging at our sides. Tuck your thumbs across your palms, then wrap the other four fingers around each thumb, forming a loose fist. Next, lightly touch the thumb side of the fist to the area near *Fengshi* point, the same as in the Taoist position.

The Closed-Fist position can be useful when one's energy is weak. Sealing in the thumb with the fingers, turns the Chi back into the related organ systems and prevents leakage. Since the thumb relates to the Lungs, this posture helps preserve and nurture our Lung Chi.

It also has a similar effect with each of the organs corresponding to the individual fingers. The middle finger relates to circulation and the Pericardium. The index finger corresponds to the Large Intestine Chi. The ring finger to the endocrine system or Triple Burner. And finally, the pinky finger corresponds to both the Heart and Small Intestine Chi.

The key to getting the most out of this position is making a firm seal of the fingers around the thumb, but *without* any of the requisite tension commonly associated with making a punching fist.

There is also another element to this type of non-martial fist which is the elongation or downward stretching of the back of the hand, as in the Beaks method. When the back of the hand is elongated, it helps form a connection to the whole arm and shoulder. A side view of the Closed-Fist position and the other Wuji hand methods may be found in the Additional Plates section.

**Wuji Posture - Closed-Fist Position**

# THE CHI ADHERES TO THE BACK

Students of the Tai Chi Classics are quite familiar with the saying, "The Chi adheres to the back." But what does it mean and why is it important in our Zhan Zhuang practice?

In terms of Zhan Zhuang, the Chi gathering and adhering to the back primarily refers to the movement of elements of Yang and Yin Chi to the region of the Governing Vessel, the spine and later, the Central Channel.

What happens with enough practice is that more and more of the 'Yin tissue' in the front of the body, that is, the chest and abdominal muscles as well as the internal tissues behind them, relax downward and back toward the spine.

This is especially true of the all-important Psoas muscles who's natural elongation as we know, is both downward *and* toward the back. When this effect occurs, the Yin tissue in front begins to feel more insubstantial, while the Yang Chi of the back becomes more tangible. This is important later when we want to create the 'Hanging Basket' effect using the Psoas muscles and the Kua for maximum suspensive relaxation.

The importance of the spine, for both health and martial achievement, cannot be over-estimated. On the health side, in addition to the nerves innervating all the organs, there is the spinal cord itself which transmits nerve messages to the brain and back into the body. On the martial arts side, those same nerves are responsible for the rapid-fire reaction and response time necessary for real life self-defense. And the spine is central to issuing powerful Jing.

As the Chi begins to 'adhere to the back,' we feel definite changes taking place in our structure. Not so much the physical structure, but rather, these changes occur in our *energy body* which becomes more clearly defined and sculpted through Zhan Zhuang. Eventually there's almost a tangible solidity to it.

So, when we first feel the Yin tissue of the abdomen and internal organs soften, and begin to empty of substantiality as the Chi makes its way to the back, this triggers, at least internally, a *very* slight shift in our weight distribution and a deeper sense of internal relaxation. As more and more of the Chi reaches the back and spine, one feels an internal strength and solidity to the entire area. It feels as though your back is like a stone wall, filled with an almost unlimited potential strength and ultra-solid stability. This stage seems to naturally manifest to some degree with enough proper Zhan Zhuang training. When it does occur, we are filled with a sense of power and emptiness which we can then utilize for healing or martial arts.

**List of Regional Correspondences**

| | |
|---|---|
| Head | Yang |
| Neck | Yang |
| Throat | Yin |
| Chest | Yin |
| Abdomen | Yin |
| Back | Yang |
| **Legs** | |
| Front | Yang |
| Back | Yang |
| Inside | Yin |
| Outside | Yang |
| **Arms** | |
| Outside | Yang |
| Inside | Yin |

## THE TRANSFORMATION PROCESS

In the old way of training, we assumed a posture and just held it, while the body endeavored to sort things out. In other words, we set up the frame of our bone structure and maintained that throughout the time of our stand, while the tissues made their adjustments. Why? "Because that's how it works." And that was basically the extent of the explanation given. Of course, it was true, but that didn't go very far in providing any understanding of the process itself.

So the question remains. What is the actual process or progression in Zhan Zhuang and how does it work? What occurs and why? The answer is multi-faceted, mainly because changes take place on so many levels, such as the physical, energetic, emotional and mental. As these changes manifest, there is a definite interrelationship that develops between them. You could call it a triggering mechanism.

For example, the release of certain physical tensions or blockages can trigger an emotional response which could be anything from mild to overwhelming.

This has to do with what's called the body's *cellular memory*, which registers and records all of our daily life experiences.

As some of these deep blockages are released and years of held tension dissolve, we sometimes feel an incredible elation, a sense of greater space within the body or an actual feeling of freedom.

But, if this blockage was part of a negative engram, that is, a negative cellular memory pattern, the same feelings that created the tension in the first place could very possibly surface and manifest just as they were, triggering a negative or uncomfortable feeling.

But not to worry. Here's where we need to use our Yi, meaning intention and will, to hang in there and let the emotions wash through us until at a certain point they run their course and dissolve into pure energy. This is then added to our body's system and recirculated.

This is one of the ways Zhan Zhuang's transformation process works and one of the reasons why Zhan Zhuang practitioners have more vitality and emotional balance than the average person.

One of my teachers once told me, it takes about three years of correct daily practice to work through most of the physical karma one has accumulated in this lifetime.

Now, let's look at things from a different perspective. Think of our ability to focus one-pointedly in the low Dan Tien, as a *magnet*. The more of our total consciousness that we can bring to bear over the years, the more powerful the magnet becomes.

And the more powerful the magnet becomes, the greater it's ability to pull into itself, focus and turn, all the 'iron filings,' meaning the energies and other elements of the body, in the same direction.

As more and more of the body becomes 'magnetized,' the greater the bio-electromagnetic charge we can bring forth and issue. In terms of health, the enhanced bio-electromagnetic charge provides additional 'Chi fuel' for the body, so it naturally runs better, longer and with fewer problems.

**The Transformational Sequence**

When one first begins training, a series of processes are initiated on multiple levels. The deep interconnections of these various levels often make it difficult at the outset to understand what's really happening. At that point, all one knows for sure is that discomfort is involved and the whole exercise is not very easy. The good news is, it *does* get easier over time. And not only that, after years of training, what used to take us thirty minutes to achieve, in terms of relaxation, can many times be accomplished in only five. That leaves us free during the rest of our standing session to enter into deeper and deeper states of relaxation. This is another way the Zhan Zhuang transformation process works.

Now, in order to shed some more light on this, we shall examine each of the interconnected levels individually. They are: the physical, energetic, emotional, mental and inevitably spiritual.

**Physical**

The physical transformation begins with the strengthening, mending and healing of the body. Any past injuries or internal blockages must be dealt with, and this can go from the skin all the way into the bones and bone marrow. As a part of all this, the body's structures realign and come into balance and one's internal organs are cleansed and repaired. As a result, many old injuries or long standing health issues can finally be resolved. *This transformation is primarily due to the enhanced Chi flow and blood circulation that develops through daily training.*

Such was the case for me. I tried nearly everything, every modality to heal my injuries. Some were useless, others did a little and a few actually made some positive changes I could feel. But it wasn't until I began daily Zhan Zhuang training, that these long standing issues were finally healed and strengthened to the point where it became almost like the problem never existed.

**Energetic**

Our energy body, of which there are several, is intimately connected to the physical body. And as such, there is a strong mutual influence. But not only is the energy body influenced by the physical, it can also be greatly influenced by our emotions and our current state of mind. Just as the physical body begins a healing process, the same is true of the energy body which has often been concurrently damaged, especially in the case of severe or long standing injuries. One of the reasons old injuries don't heal is precisely because the Chi energy has also been altered or deformed by the original trauma.

So along with the physical, our energy body also undergoes a similar healing transformation. When this has progressed to a certain degree the result is a definite increase in Chi flow, the benefits of which are passed onto the body. This transformation also affects our emotions.

**Emotions**

Impressions of every event in our lives are stored in the body's cellular memory as well as in certain parts of the body itself. This includes deep emotional moments and events of both a positive and negative nature. It is primarily the intense negative emotional experiences that we are concerned with. For if not loosened and resolved, they will plague the individual for their entire life.

This is where Zhan Zhuang can *really* help. You see, as part of the Zhan Zhuang process, we eventually make greater and greater contact with the subconscious, which is where most of these deep feelings have been hidden and stored.

As the organs are cleansed, according to Taoist theory, certain emotions are also brought to the surface where they can finally be processed and resolved. Below is a list of correspondences between the five Yin Organs and their linked negative emotions. This is a very simplified breakdown.

## ORGAN AND EMOTION CORRESPONDENCES

| Liver | Anger |
|---|---|
| Heart | Impatience |
| Spleen | Worry |
| Lungs | Sadness |
| Kidneys | Fear |

Of course *fear*, housed in the Kidneys, is the *root* of all the other negative emotions. Conquer our fears, our whole world changes.

### Mind

Just as the energy body influences the physical, so do the mind and certain repetitive thoughts that act upon the emotions which in turn can affect the organs and at times the whole body. Under certain conditions this influence also works in the opposite direction, that is the emotions influencing the mind. The extent of the mind's influence on all the other systems cannot be overestimated. Witness the Yogi's abilities to absolutely control and alter many of the body's vital functions. If you‘re doing it right, how this works in Zhan Zhuang is at first more indirect. Rather than confront certain types of negative thought sequences directly, by concentrating on developing our single-pointed focus, this sort of material is brought out and dissolved of itself.

### Spirit

As a result of this physical, energetic, emotional and mental cleansing, the total human being goes through what often may be a profound awakening in perception. With the mind calm and the emotions more placid, one's point of view naturally begins to evolve and change. Depending on how far one takes Zhan Zhuang training over the years, it becomes possible to experience various ‘little enlightenments’ which open the different psychic and spiritual centers in the body.

## WORKING WITH PHYSICAL DYNAMIC TENSIONS

Our Central Equilibrium and upright body balance are dependent to a large extent on the equalization of two opposing forces, the force of gravity, the descending Heaven energy, and the rising Earth energy.

If either of these is too much or too little, pressure imbalances manifest in the body.

Of these, especially as one gets older, the force of gravity begins to take its toll and many suffer from compression of some sort. Compression by it's nature, reduces space in the body.

This is the complete antithesis of what we want in Zhan Zhuang. So, what to do?

From the overview, the answer lies in sinking the Chi so that the Earth energy can freely rise and bolster our Upright Chi. But before this can happen, we must find a way to balance the opposing forces, such that the constricted regions are freed up and allowed to function properly.

The idea is to first use our peripheral feeling-awareness during Zhan Zhuang meditation to become conscious of the locations in the body that seem blocked or tight, or just plain odd. If you 'listen,' the body will tell you because as we know, the body's prime directive is to heal itself.

Once some of these regions have been located, we will pick one, usually the worst in terms of pain or discomfort. Depending on it's specific location, we will work with the region or 'Station' above and below the suspect area first. The idea of Stations is discussed next.

**The Station Method**

The idea of 'Stations' is quite simple. If we think of a painful area as being damned up, then in the region above the dam, 'water' backs up, and in the region below the dam, 'water' can't get through. By working with the regions above and below, we can in effect, break down the dam and restore the free flow. In this example we will use the Wuji posture and the elbow as the problem region.

1) The first step is to place our attention on our shoulder area, (the Station above) and work on surrendering it to gravity or the descending force. This means to allow the muscles of the shoulder and the upper arm to elongate and relax downward. This alone can sometimes be enough to release the blockage.

2) If the above action didn't completely resolve the issue, the next step is to relax deep into the elbow. Try to feel into the dead center of it.

3) Next, immediately proceed to the Stations below, that is, the forearm and wrist and feel them elongate.

By releasing in this manner, there is an opening and lengthening created from the shoulder, down through the elbow and into the forearm, wrist and hand. This elongation should provide greater ease of movement as well as a larger pain-free range of motion.

For a lower body example, let's say we have an ankle problem.

1) Begin with the Station above, which is the knee. Work on relaxing the entire knee area, the front, back, inside and outside.

2) Next, release all the muscles between the knee joint and the ankle. This region is divided into four compartments. The Anterior

compartment in front, the Lateral compartment on the side and the Posterior and Deep Posterior compartments in the back.

3) Now, relax all parts of the ankle.

4) Finally, try to relax all parts of the foot. The top, the inside, the outside and the all-important bottom of the foot. In this case, try to feel as much tension and weight as possible, empty into and *out of* the bottom of the foot.

This method can work with almost any location in the body. If the problem lies in the hip, then we could use the midriff above and the knee below. And so on...

Sometimes however, with severe or long term problems even after all the above procedures, there can still be something wrong. So, the next step is to find a way to deeply release the problem region itself. This involves using the mind.

**A Nei Kung Method**
In this technique we use the energy body and our feeling-awareness.

1) Think of the elbow again. Move your feeling-awareness into the dead center of the elbow joint and imagine a tiny sphere at that point.

2) Next, feel that the tiny sphere grows until it fills the entire elbow joint. As this occurs, sensations of both downward and upward releases can be felt.

3) Now, again bring your attention to the center of the elbow, but this time try to be aware and 'feel' two spheres, the tiny one in the center and the fully expanded one, filling the joint.

4) Lastly, let the little sphere fully expand as before, but this time, keep a chunk of your peripheral feeling-awareness on the already expanded sphere as well.

When done correctly the feelings of multidirectional release will extend beyond the arm into the torso and back.

All these methods have worked primarily with the descending Heaven energy where there is an upward compression such as is common with a 'frozen' shoulder and many other types of muscular injuries.

But there are occasions where there is too much downward compression. In other words too much descending energy. In these cases we must relieve the overbearing downward pressure with the rising, lifting Earth energy.

This can sometimes be as simple as let's say, physically lifting the chest off the Solar Plexus and upper abdomen. This type of compression is common among people who spend large amounts of time peering at a computer screen.

Unfortunately certain types of downward problems such as flaccidity or atrophy cannot be solved so simply. These require much dedicated Zhan Zhuang training such that we can *truly* sink the Chi and by doing so activate the more delicate rising Yin Earth Chi. This lifting energy will then over time gradually tighten such things as overstretched tendons and atrophied muscles. The thing to know about the rising energy is that it must almost always be used in concert with the descending force in order to maintain a proper balance. In other words we must be able to be aware of both the Heaven and Earth energies and lead or follow them simultaneously.

# WORKING WITH ARM POSTURES

## EIGHT POSTURES FOR MARTIAL ARTS

This is a basic postural sequence to develop internal martial power. By examining the order of progression, we observe that we start roughly in the area of the middle Dan Tien, then take the energy down to the low Dan Tien, then up to the upper Dan Tien area. From there we move back down to the low Dan Tien in stages, projecting energy outward, expanding laterally (splitting the body) and finally grounding and storing the energy accumulated in practice, while at the same time venting any excess or unwanted Chi down and out the bottoms of the feet, back into the Earth. (see photo sequence)

What we see in the cumulative progression is the establishment of various circles, cylinders and most importantly, spheres within the body, each cultivating specific energies as well as overall body energy.

This brings me to a point about health. Internal martial practices such as these are generally far more extensive in both scope and time required than the material used solely for health. For example, those applying these methods for health generally train for about 20-40 minutes a session.

On the other hand, those wishing to achieve real martial power, train Zhan Zhuang for 60 minutes at a time, and often repeat this twice during the day. And it is this additional training, which at least in part creates the side-effect of a healthy body for internal martial artists.

The following sequence comes through the Han brothers lineage. *Han Xing Qiao* and his younger brother, *Han Xing Yuan* were two of *Wang Xiang Zhai's* earliest students.

**Posture 1 - Holding The Ball, Embracing The Tree**
This is *the* basic Zhan Zhuang posture. It is the essence of the practice and can be used all by itself to great efficacy. It can also be considered a microcosm of all other arm postures and is extremely useful in cultivating whole body spherical energy in later stages of practice.

**Posture 2 - Dropping The Energy Down**
This posture takes the energy cultivated in the first position and directs it downward. It is especially useful for emptying energy from the chest, Solar Plexus and abdomen. Eventually this becomes the ability to circulate everything downward throughout the body and into the ground.

**Posture 3 - Cultivating The Low Dan Tien**
This position directly cultivates the low Dan Tien, and as such, the tendency can be to collapse part of our alignment due to the overwhelming downward energetic inclination of the arms. This is best counteracted by lifting and opening the spine. In other words, balancing the descending Heaven energy with the ascending Earth energy, which is one of the ultimate goals in standing practice.

**Posture 4 - Returning To Origin**
Turning the palms to face the low Dan Tien accomplishes two things. Like posture two, it empties the Chi downward but also helps to return the Chi to it's origin, in this case the low Dan Tien, the center of physical power, the source of health and martial strength.

**Posture 5 - Cultivating The Upper Dan Tien**
This begins cultivation of the upper Dan Tien and it's eventual hardwiring linkage to the low and middle Dan Tiens. It also has the effect of opening and lengthening the body vertically and helps develop the top portion of the whole body sphere.

**Posture 6 - Projecting Out Through The Hands**

This position opens and prepares the body for the projection of energy through the arms and out through the fingers. Often this is combined with focusing the eyes far into the distance, like out to the horizon. This trains and aids in the projection of Chi. For healing, we can reverse the direction of the flow by inhaling, that is drawing energy into the body from a great distance and then using it to augment and restore our Chi.

**Posture 6a - Variation**

This is a Bagua style variation I learned. Instead of projecting energy out, it pulls the upper Dan Tien energy cultivated in posture five, down into the middle and later the low Dan Tien. Eventually, this posture generates spiral energy both coming in and going out of the body.

**Posture 7 - Cultivating Middle Balance**

This position is unique among the eight in that it's halfway between the highest and lowest arm positions. It is interesting to note that the late disciple of *Wang Xiang Zhai*, *Peng Si Yu* taught only one of the eight postures and it was this one. Posture seven has the ability to cultivate the middle and the central balance. Energetically, it contains elements of both the higher and lower arm positions.

**Posture 8 - Emptying Into The Earth**

This is the ending posture of the sequence and for good reason. Often during practice, especially after much training, the body can temporarily absorb and circulate far more energy than can be safely contained or utilized during it's everyday function. Some of this new energy is absorbed into the fascia or bone marrow for future use, but the rest can become dangerous if left unattended in the body. Posture eight provides an outlet to return any excess Chi that can't be safely stored, back into the Earth and out into the atmosphere.

**Posture 1**

**Posture 2**

**Posture 3**

**Posture 4**

**Posture 5**

**Posture 6**

**Posture 6a**

**Posture 7**

**Posture 8**

## FOUR POSTURES FOR HEALTH AND HEALING

This sequence was developed by *Wang Xiang Zhai* and his disciple, Dr. *Hu*. It came about as a result of the government forbidding Wang and many others from teaching martial arts during the Cultural Revolution period. Thank goodness the authorities finally came to their senses.

According to Wang, this method was developed through trial and error in which it was determined that the following four posture sequence was the most effective for health and healing of the body.

I can personally attest to it's healing power. Some years back I had a severe allergic reaction. It was so bad that I was bedridden for a while. When I finally began to recover, about the only thing I could do was Wuji standing meditation. This began the strengthening process and allowed me to shortly begin using Wang's four posture health sequence.

Imagine my surprise when upon completing my first session, I found a profound leap in my overall energy and well-being. As a result, after a week of twenty minute training sessions (5 minutes per posture) my energy level basically returned to normal.

Please note that when practicing for health it is permissible and often preferable to train with the eyes closed. The purpose of this is to help keep the Chi energy focused inwardly for healing.

In the four posture health method, the first and fourth postures will look familiar in that they are basically the same as postures one and eight of the martial sequence. The second and third postures however are different and fulfill unique purposes. (see photo sequence)

**Posture 1 - Create The Microcosm**
Although looking outwardly the same as it's martial arts counterpart, posture one is in fact used somewhat differently in that we employ it to gather and at the same time mobilize the body's Chi for healing circulation.

Please be aware that the hand and arm placement in posture one can be anywhere from just below the Throat Notch to just above the Solar Plexus. Often when one is weak it is best not to raise the arms too high at first. Remember, the higher we raise the arms, the more we exercise the Heart. But there is a time and place for this.

**Posture 2 - Support The Sky**
And that time is posture number two. On the surface it looks like we're raising the arms to head level, which of course we are. The trick here is to cause the Heart Chi to descend in spite of this. Healthy Chi in the Heart channel flows downward from the armpit to the pinky finger.

The way to do this is to simultaneously relax and release all the chest and abdominal muscles downward, as the hands are raised to the level of the ears. When you can maintain this through the length of time in the posture, you will be exercising the Heart without taxing it too much. Actually you will be relaxing it through the downward released chest muscles and descending Chi flow, while working it at the same time. (the arms held high)

Sounds like a bit of a paradox. Well, you might as well get used to it. One doesn't get very far in the advanced practices if they can't encompass paradoxes.

**Posture 3 - Stand In the Stream**
This position now takes the energy accumulated in posture one and

raised up in posture two, both downward and outward. The downward part is obvious. The hands were at head level and now they're at the sides of the body, at the level of the floating rib, if possible.

The arm position demonstrated here is the advanced one, with the tips of the elbows facing directly down toward the ground. It takes a lot of openness in the shoulders, chest and upper back to relax in this manner.

The position of the arms in this posture also creates the potential effect of redistributing our body weight. We call this 'splitting the body,' that is, emptying the Central Channel region which generates a feeling of no weight along the centerline or central-cylinder. It does this by activating the Left and Right Chi Kung Channels as well as the Yang and Yin Heel and Linking Channels. In other words, redistributing the weight through the Left and Right Channels facilitates a better free-flow of Chi through the all-important Central Channel because there is less, and eventually no resistance to impede it. Please note, the activation of the Left and Right presupposes the interaction of the Heel and Linking Channels which oversee large quantities of Chi.

**Posture 4 - Store And Release**

This position basically fulfills the same purpose as it's martial counterpart. It allows excess energy to drain out through the pores of the skin, as well as into the ground. In some cases, this excess energy may contain toxic or harmful Chi. Once this cleansing is accomplished, one stores energy in the low Dan Tien before finishing. Eventually at a more advanced level, one can release and store at the same time. At an even more advanced level one's root will have made contact deep within the Earth. This creates the possibility of receiving and absorbing the powerful healing Earth Chi which rises up directly into the body through the feet.

**Posture 1**

**Posture 2**

**Posture 3**

**Posture 4**

## INTERNAL ORGAN POSTURES

In this section we introduce some of the many postures to benefit the five Yin Organs. These are the Liver, Heart, Spleen, Lung and Kidneys. I once asked one of my teachers, who knew nearly 400 standing postures from a number of traditions, which ones were the absolute best for nurturing and rejuvenating the five Yin Organs and the result was the following five postures. (see photo sequence)

### Liver Posture

This is a deceptively simple posture with very sophisticated underpinnings. First one must find *Qimen* point, LIV-14, located two ribs below the nipple in the 6th Intercostal space. This extremely powerful point is a masterpoint for the health of the Liver. Opening it breaks up stagnant Liver Chi and blood, the insidious cause of many maladies. In this posture, the edge of the hand is lined up with *Qimen* point while the angle of the forearm follows the shape of the space between the ribs and is inclined very slightly downward.

### Heart Posture

In this posture we line up the hands roughly on either side of *Shanzhong* point, CV-17, known as the residence of Ancestral Chi. This point is located on the midline of the Sternum, between the nipples, level with the 4th Intercostal space and directly effects both circulation and respiration. It also effects the Pericardium protective energy around the Heart. By opening the armpit, keeping the shoulders and elbows down, and the inside of the forearms, wrists and palms relaxed, we cause the Heart Chi to descend and circulate properly.

### Spleen Posture

This position is the same as for the Liver. When I asked my teacher about that, he pointed to the Middle *Jiao*. What he meant was that there is a deeply interconnected relationship between the Liver and Spleen. Put simply, the free flow of Liver Chi strongly influences the proper functioning of the Spleen and when excessive, can easily disrupt it during the digestive operations of the Middle *Jiao*.

There is also another reason for the duplicity. The Liver and Spleen are located roughly on the same horizontal plane. And since there is a *Qimen* point both on the right (the Liver side) and the left (the Spleen side) this posture serves both. It's where you put your Yi and feeling-awareness that directs the energy more to one than the other.

Also, it's useful to take note of another point in the region. And that is *Zhangmen* LIV-13, a very important Spleen point *residing* on the Liver channel. *Zhangmen* (System's Door) is located just below the 11th floating rib on each side. It is through this point that the Liver Chi passes en route to *Qimen* LIV-14 and the Liver and Spleen organs themselves. Please note, in Chinese Medicine and Taoist theory the concept of the Spleen *also includes the functions of the Pancreas*.

**Lung Posture**
By extending the arms out to the sides, we naturally stretch the rib cage which makes more space for the Lungs to breathe deeply. In addition, by opening the Shoulder's Nests, we activate *Zhongfu* LU-1, the origin point of the Lung meridian. This opening needs to be strongly downward as well as lateral. There are a number of variations for this posture, mostly based on which way the palms are facing. Palms up, as in the photos, palms down, facing the ground, palms facing outward and palms facing backward. It is important to keep all the tissue through which the Lung meridian passes relaxed at all times. In the palms up photo example, this means completely releasing the chest downward while opening the shoulder blades and back and absorbing more of the arm weight there.

**Kidney Posture**

This position is quite different from all the other organ postures and as such, requires some very unique alignments and adjustments. The reason for this is the location of the Kidneys and a different way to open the back.

Put your elbows a fair distance away from the sides of the torso, while letting the forearms dangle, fingers pointing to the ground.

Next, as you close your shoulders, lift your elbows, wrists and hands as one unit and role everything backwards and down.

So, the sequence is, 'up, back and down.' If done correctly the elbow tips should be behind the midline of the torso or better yet completely behind the torso itself.

All this sounds simple enough but there is one thing to watch out for. Under no circumstances should we let our chest stick out. This is a natural consequence if the elbows are pushed far enough behind the body.

So, in order to avoid this pitfall, we can gently lift the chest and abdomen when we do the 'up' part of the three phase sequence. While doing this, breathe fully up under the Clavicle and continue inhaling as you move through the 'back' phase.

Now, in the 'down' phase, release the whole front of the chest, torso, and abdomen *downward* as you release the shoulder blades and arms, down the back. When done right, there will be a stretch to the chest and a sinking, but not a bowing or arching out.

**Liver Posture**

**Heart Posture**

**Spleen Posture**

**Lung Posture**

**Kidney Posture**

## TWO TAI CHI CULTIVATION POSTURES

In traditional Tai Chi training, a number of postures besides the Wuji posture of Commencement were used for standing cultivation practice. These include the familiar 'Bird's Tail' movements *Peng*, *Lu*, *Ji* and *An* plus *Dan Pien* - Single Whip.

Besides these, it is highly advised that the serious Tai Chi martial artist incorporate the power of Zhan Zhuang into their training.

Here is an easy way to combine Zhan Zhuang *with* your form. Simply execute your form as usual but when you get to the end point of each posture, simply stop and maintain that position anywhere from one to three breaths and then continue to the end point of the next posture and do the same.

This should first be done at the end point of each posture, meaning the fully opened posture. Once this is comfortable, one can add the transitions between postures to the regime. Believe me, this practice will literally transform your form.

If nothing else, it will open and balance one's postures, allowing greater fluidity and Chi flow. After achieving this, one's Tai Chi will jump to a whole new level.

Since many readers will be familiar with Tai Chi's most basic postures, I have decided to present two additional Tai Chi cultivation postures they might not know about.

These two postures can be used to cultivate all the basic energies of Tai Chi. (see photo sequence)

The first is done in the standard forward Bow Stance. The second utilizes a back-weighted Bow-Stance such as found in *Lu*, Rollback.

The first posture requires quite a lot of flexibility to execute fully and so is often begun with a far less pronounced stretch of the back arm.

The amazing thing about this posture is that as the body hollows and opens up, it does so in a manner that naturally generates *spiral energy*. The potential for spiral energy actually comes from the unwinding of the tautly stretched tissue, especially in the hips and Kua.

The second posture further unwinds the tissues from the previous posture and allows the Chi flow to become as open as possible. In addition, the position of the back arm facilitates a connection with the Heaven Chi, which at later stages, can be drawn in and passed through the body.

Just as with the back arm, the front arm has its unique function. It can be called the 'offering hand' as if reaching out and offering your hand to someone. Only this extension should be felt internally, more in the energy body than in the physical. Once done right, one feels a continuous flow of Chi passing in and out of the body.

The more one becomes an empty vessel or a clear channel in these postures, the greater flow of Chi the body can pass through or *issue*.

The usual method is sixty minutes. Fifteen minutes front stance, fifteen minutes back stance and then change sides. Of course as with all new postures, you can always start with less time for each and work your way up.

**Tai Chi Cultivation Posture - Front-Weighted**

**Tai Chi Cultivation Posture - Back-Weighted**

**Front-Weighted - Side View**

**Back-Weighted - Side View**

## SINGLE-WEIGHTED STANCES

Single-weighted stances are considered advanced and should not be attempted until one has a firm understanding of the basics. I stood in equal-weighted, parallel stances for a couple of years before I was ready to derive any real benefit from these. (see photos)

As with the feet parallel stances, single-weighted stances also have many variations, most of which can be seen on the internet. For our example, I have chosen a basic single-weighted posture to illustrate the differences compared to the equal-weighted stances.

First, let's examine the position of the feet in relationship to one another. The channel or width between the two feet can range from no channel, meaning both heels on a single line, all the way out to hip width. A channel width of one fist's distance is often used.

The second thing we must consider is the angle the two feet create. Since the front leg is almost always facing straight ahead, this angle is determined by the turnout of the rear foot. This can be anything from ninety degrees to zero degrees. (both feet facing straight ahead) A thirty to forty-five degree turnout of the rear foot is often a good place to start.

The next thing we need to look at is the height of the raised heel of the front foot. The distance off the ground can vary from just the width of a piece of paper, to four or five inches. This latter, where only the ball of the foot is touching, requires a vertical stretch of the Kua and torso in order to be effective. This increased verticality necessitates an even greater refinement in balance. This also manifests as a clearer differentiation between substantial and insubstantial.

And lastly, the length between the front and back foot must be examined. This distance can be anywhere from the 'heel to toe line,' that is, the heel of the front foot on a horizontal line with the big toe of the back foot, to the front foot being twelve to eighteen inches ahead. Normally it is best not to stretch this distance out too much, especially if the Kua is tight, or you will run into alignment problems with the hips and knees.

The first thing we feel when we assume a single-weighted stance is the need for a much finer balance and hence, even greater relaxation. But the main difference can be found in the posture itself. Notice the difference between the two arms and the clear division of weight in the legs, ascribed to each.

Instead of both arms being held in the same manner as with the feet-parallel, equal-weighted postures, in the single-weighted stances, the 'back' arm and palm, associated with the weighted leg, tilt slightly downward, while the front arm and hand, associated with the empty or less weighted leg, scoop slightly upward. Therefore, the front leg and arm embrace the insubstantiality of Yin, while the back leg and arm encompass the substantiality of Yang.

Also, there is an important interconnection between the slightly down-turned palm and the heel of the weighted leg. They both sink the Chi and root the descending Heaven energy, down under the foot. On the other hand, the scooped arm and *Yongquan* point, K-1 on the heel-raised front foot, do just the opposite. They both cause the ascending Earth energy to lift or rise.

From this we see the potential of these types of postures to create a balanced interchange of both the descending *Yang* Chi and the ascending *Yin* Chi.

Of course, this also occurs with the equal weighted stances, but not exactly in the same manner.

The difference is, with single-weighted stances, the delineation is more distinct. Half the body does one thing, while the other half does something else. This is in essence, the definition of Tai Chi. Half the body Yin, absorbing, diverting, while the other half is Yang, expanding, issuing. These two then exchange in the continuous unending cycle we call *Tai Chi*.

In the last set of photos we examine a variation requiring an even finer balance thread. This method is particularly effective if one is intent on being a good kicker. The idea is to step things up a notch by keeping one foot in the air, anywhere from just barely off the ground to leg parallel to the ground and everywhere in between.

This is a highly difficult, advanced technique that often makes a practitioner of many years feel like a rank beginner, both in terms of the refined balance necessary and also leg strength. These stances offer the clearest differentiation between substantiality and insubstantiality, especially in the legs.

**Single-Weighted Stance - Front View**

**Side View**

**Leg Lift - Low**

**Leg Lift - Medium**

## THE SANTI POSTURE

"The *Santi* posture is an excellent adjunct to the Zhan Zhuang standing postures of *Yiquan* and Tai Chi Chuan. It is the primary standing posture used by *Xingyi* practitioners and there is a reason for this.

The Santi posture is based on the metal element in the *Xingyi* five element fists. The metal element corresponds to the Lungs. Therefore by cultivating in this posture the Lungs and the *Kong Chi* are greatly enhanced.

Another aspect is the actual positioning and weighting of the posture. In practical terms the posture itself provides a clear physical and energetic protection of one's centerline. (see photos)

Traditionally the division of weight between the feet is 40/60 or 30/70 back-weighted. This fact of itself generates a very condensed and powerful form of Yang Chi.

When asked what techniques he used in combat, *Wang Xiang Zhai* said he used *Bagua* footwork, Tai Chi neutralizing and diverting, and *Xingyi* power for attack.

Begin with your feet together. Turn your left foot out about 45 degrees and then step straight ahead with your right foot to a distance of two or two-and-a-half times your foot's length. To do this, place the heel of the right foot where the toe was, do that again, and then half as much again.

This longer posture helps distribute the weight in the correct manner. Although 40/60 weighting is considered standard, for the new learner sometimes a 50/50 weight distribution can be a good place to start.

The next thing we want to be aware of is the Kua. The Kua should be almost squared to the front but not 100%, although in some Xingyi styles it *is* done that way.

According to Sun Lu Tang the idea with the back leg is to create a linkage from below the Lateral Malleolus up through the hip. Also make sure the weight dropping down into the back foot is coming from the torso, Dan Tien and Kua.

For the front leg we want to feel as though the knee, and especially *Heding* point is being screwed or spiraled into the ground. This should feel completely vertical even though there is actually a slight physical angle. *Heding* point is located just above the kneecap.

Now as to the arms and spacing. One way to approach this is to do each arm separately. Let your left (back) arm hang freely and then open your shoulder blade. Slightly rotate the elbow away from the body and allow the forearm to also come out and feel supported from underneath. Finally, point the thumb to the navel area. You don't want this arm too far away from the body, but you also don't want it touching.

For the right or lead arm, begin with the arm hanging freely. This time while opening from the spine and shoulder blade, swing the elbow and forearm up, *under* and forward so that the wrist is at the same height as the shoulder.

Ideally the tip of the elbow is facing straight down and you want to feel the index finger pointing straight up. The elbow joint itself should be aligned with the front knee. The arm should feel 'fully' extended and yet not. It's a bit of a dichotomy, but that's how it's described.

*When done correctly you will feel the same verticality with your index finger, the tip of the extended right elbow, and Heding point*. Use the energetic connection between the vertical index finger and *Heding* point to root your alignments.

If your neck is aligned with the center of your torso, it will be slightly facing toward the left. Now pivot the neck until your eyes focus on the 'Tiger's Mouth' opening of the front hand. Here it is important to note that we should not extend the front arm too far because it will lead to the disintegration of our structural integrity.

To form the 'Tiger's Mouth,' first elongate the hand. Next stretch the thumb away from the index finger, then pull the index finger back so it points straight up.

Now with the basic alignments in place, we will use the principle of condensing and telescoping the joints inward, and then dropping everything out the back and down the rear leg as we open up. When done correctly this should lift the energy up and over into the right hip, and from there down under the front foot.

As to further extension of the front arm. If there's a feeling of space in the shoulder or shoulder-blade area, simply extend the arm a little further, paying attention that none of the muscles around the shoulder blade are being lifted. This also goes for the Pectoralis Major and Minor muscles in the chest. All these regions should feel like they're still sinking.

With the *Santi* posture as with all the other postures, eventually an open Channel develops. In this case the Channel has a sensation of feeling narrower when compared with the feet-parallel Zhan Zhuang stance. This is due to the position of the legs and torso.

The next thing that will happen with continued practice is a feeling of the body 'splitting' or dividing. This is sometimes called the separation of Yang and Yin. This is where one half of the body does one thing while the other half does another. In the Santi posture the back leg and arm are rooting and condensing while the front leg and arm are opening and expanding. These movements follow a variation of the Macrocosmic full body circulation pathway as described below.

Chi from the rear foot goes up into the low Dan Tien, then down under the front foot, and finally back up the spine and out the palm of the lead hand. Simultaneously as the Chi goes up the back to the shoulder-blade and *Dazhui* region, it also descends under the rear foot and rear palm, creating a powerful root.

Try this. Assume the *Santi* posture. Now incline the torso a little forward, keeping everything straight from the top of the head to the tailbone. Next let the tailbone sink down and *then* under. (tailbone tuck) This drives the weight down, under and forward while simultaneously straightening the spine back up to vertical.

In the *Santi* posture careful attention should also be paid to the neck. Following *Xingyi* basics, the neck should feel clearly extended or elongated, and yet at the same time feel released or at least not tightly bound to the shoulder-tops and torso. Also the chin must be gently tucked in order to help protect the throat. Lastly, the focus of the eyes through the Tiger's Mouth gap should be either a few feet away or better yet, far out onto the horizon."

For those interested in exploring *Santi* further, there is a stepping method used by *Xingyi* practitioners to rapidly enter into the posture. Video of this procedure is readily available on the internet.

**Santi Posture**

**Side View**

# WORKING WITH IMBALANCES

## AS THE WATER SETTLES, THE ROCKS APPEAR

This Zen saying means that once the novice first starts to become comfortable in their Zhan Zhuang training, certain problems of which they were previously unaware, surface and make themselves known. As the water settles, the rocks appear.

The first thing people generally feel when they begin standing are various 'discomforts' in the physical body. These imbalances are generated by causes such as old injuries, energetic blockages, including organ or gland imbalances, psychic or emotional karma, and general mental rigidity.

In this discussion we will primarily focus on the physical arena as these issues must be reckoned with before the other areas become steadily accessible. So what is it exactly that causes our discomfort and pain and perhaps more importantly, how do we change it and become relaxed?

It can be said that all discomfort within the body is caused by incorrect tension between two primary dynamic forces - the descending Heaven energy (gravity, sinking, Yang) and the ascending Earth energy. (lifting, rising, Yin)

These can be thought of as opposite pressures which when not properly equalized, create pain, discomfort or at the very least odd feelings or sensations in the body. These pressures manifest both physically and energetically. Our goal here is to enable a balanced interchange.

Following the laws of hydrodynamics (the study of fluids in motion) we can postulate that an imbalance of pressure - either too much or too little - exerted on liquid within a defined, somewhat flexible membrane (the body) creates actual physical distortions. Eventually these can become ingrained and also warp the energy body.

As these imbalances become habitual, the body adapts and creates a 'new normal.' The definition of 'normal' in this case being what we accept as natural for us, such that no area of the body calls attention to itself. In the case of an injury, normal refers to how things felt before the damage.

Of course the new normal is actually an aberrated pattern. This means that after a time we 'get used' to the imbalance and begin to experience it as normal.

The body is often miraculous in it's ability to self-heal and yet this same adaptive ability can also be a double-edged sword, in that what can't be corrected by the body's self-healing, eventually gets blotted out of the conscious mind and feeling whenever possible.

When this occurs, the pattern has been locked into the subconscious. And that's where Zhan Zhuang can be most helpful.

The continuous practice of the standing exercise reveals these deviated subconscious patterns and eventually helps resolve them. The more years we stand, the more of these patterns emerge and are dissolved until eventually the whole human organism has been cleansed, healed and balanced.

This doesn't mean that everything's perfect from then on. On the contrary, each day we must apply our Kung Fu, that is, perseverance, time and effort, in order to regain and refine this hard won state of balanced equilibrium.

## SENSATIONS EXPERIENCED DURING THE STAND

There are many sensations experienced during Zhan Zhuang. These fall into three categories; pleasant, unpleasant and what we'll call 'odd.' The pleasant aspect will be covered later in the section, Positive Sensations - Confirmatory Signs. So for now, let us examine the more seamy side, the side that for one reason or another acts as a gate to keep out all but the most dedicated.

**Sweat**

Sweating is one of the first and most common sensations we encounter when we take up standing meditation. Sweat naturally appears when the body gets overheated. There are a number of reasons for this, but at the beginning, they relate mostly to hidden or perhaps not so hidden body tensions. This can be as simple as the fact that most people are not used to standing still for very long. Also, like learning any new physical skill, we tend to use too many muscles and often too much mental focus. These two factors always create excess tension in the body.

The other reason for this occurrence is internal organ imbalances. When organs are not functioning optimally, they tire more easily and cannot adequately support the body's systems as they try to adapt to the exercise.

For example, people with Heart problems will tend to sweat on the forehead, face and neck and perhaps the chest. Those with Kidney problems often find sweat first in the lower back and legs.

However, this is somewhat of an oversimplification in that severe deficiency in either of these organ systems can easily cause the sweat to become systemic, that is, all over the body.

Another way to figure out which organs are the cause, is to notice if the sweat is more profuse along the lines of any particular meridians.

**Heat**

Whenever we perform any strenuous physical activity long enough, our metabolic rate increases and our heartbeat speeds up. All this generates heat of one kind or another.

Also, we often find that various Chi imbalances will cause the body to get very hot as the 'impurities' are being burned off. This type of Chi rebalancing can take days, weeks, months or even years if the imbalances are severe enough.

That brings us to another important area for discussion, the location of the heat. The general rule is: 'Keep the head cool and the feet warm.' This means we want to keep the excess heat in the lower abdomen, legs and feet and avoid it pooling in the head, neck or chest.

Accumulation of excess Chi in the head or chest can have consequences if not dealt with, especially if the condition persists. Fortunately these manifestations of heat are *usually* only a wake-up call that there may be something going on.

Lastly, it is important to note that many heat conditions can often come up and then just go away later in your standing session or shortly thereafter. If this occurs, you're in luck, because you just burned out some blockages and strengthened and balanced some Chi flows.

**Cold**

In the situation just described, afterwards one sometimes feels a gentle coolness were their excess heat once was. When this happens we can also feel cool on the outside and the perfect body temperature on the inside. This is many times a lukewarm feeling, such that we almost don't feel it, as is the case within the body, when things are running really right.

Now, cold has another meaning and this has to do with circulation or in this instance, the lack of it. If there are certain parts of the body that are clearly colder than the rest, you can be sure that at least local circulation is impaired. If it is only local, then many times one will feel an increase in the local temperature by the end of the exercise.

As with heat, long standing cold problems tend to be more systemic in nature. These often relate to *Xu*, deficient conditions in the Heart, Liver, or Kidneys, but can also be caused by any of the other organs including the Triple Burner or endocrine system. With these forms of cold, it can often take a fair amount of time before there is a noticeable improvement. But if one persists in their practice, it *will* happen.

**Numbness**

In traditional Chinese Medicine, numbness is caused by dampness, either local, internal or external, or possibly a combination of all three. It is also caused by a severe restriction of Chi flow which is often the case for people with tight shoulders, lower back, hips and legs.

One of my teachers once told me, "Sometimes it's okay for the whole body to go numb during a Zhan Zhuang session." I have personally experienced a number of problem areas in the body react in this manner.

Now, there are two basic types of numbness and it is important to distinguish between them. The first is the external, musculoskeletal type caused by excess tension, essentially tight muscles and sinews or by long term deficiency due to old injuries. The second type is internal and results from dampness in the organs, often times, the Spleen, which is most susceptible. Deficient Spleen Chi due to dampness might manifest as general tiredness, along with the numbness when you stand.

**Shaking**

Shaking is another sensation often encountered the outset of Zhan Zhuang training. It is one of the processes the body uses to rebalance the dynamic tension of muscles, tendons and ligaments. If you've had broken bones, that can also be the cause. In rare cases, shaking can also signal an organ imbalance or be triggered by severe mental tension or emotional stress.

Problems in the muscles usually manifest as twitching or spasms that come and go. If the blockage is in the tendons or ligaments, the shaking can be far more violent. This generally manifests as a sort of up and down motion, an uncontrollable compression and expansion that can range from a few inches to a whole limb or more.

For some there is a stigma regarding 'the shakes.' They believe its shows a person is not at a very high level. But this is not necessarily so, in fact until a person can relax and release enough for at least some shaking to occur, they are actually holding and stuffing, either consciously or subconsciously, a mountain full of tension.

That said, as stated earlier, some people have more tolerance and ability to endure discomfort or pain than others. The key to this is, the sooner you let go, the sooner blockages are resolved and the sooner you really *do* move on to higher levels.

The process of shaking is essentially a dance between the brain and various muscles or sinews that are trying to return to their original matrix, which they have lost due to kinesthetic muscle amnesia - forgetting their normal function, how they should act.

This forgetting is often the result of old injuries where circulation has broken down, and/or where other parts of the body have taken on extra duties in an effort to help relieve an injured area. If these injuries don't heal properly, this altered behavior creates a new normal and the original patterns of say for example, the order of the nerves firing, are forgotten. That is, until we step onto the mat and train Zhan Zhuang.

**Discomfort and Pain**

These are the body's signals that tell us something is off. Discomfort will be experienced in nearly every part of the body at one time or another over the many years of Zhan Zhuang training. This can be from old problems, something recent or it could even be 'man-made,' in other words, one's structural alignment is consistently off.

This is often the case at the outset. We think it's right, it feels right, but it's not. For those fortunate enough to have consistent access to a good teacher, this will generally not be too much of a problem because most of the structural potential for problems will be seen and adjusted.

Outright pain on the other hand, is something that must not be ignored. There are many different types of pain such as stingy, achy, sharp, stabbing, twisting, oppressive and others. Each of these can have a different meaning as well as different causes or origins.

The easiest way to look at it is to divide pain into two categories, Chi stagnation and Blood stagnation. Chi stagnation is said to be energetically, the more superficial of the two, but that doesn't mean the pain cannot be intense.

With Blood stagnation on the other hand, the pain is always intense, usually sharp or stabbing. Also, *the pain seems to always be in one location*. With Chi stagnation, *the pain often moves around* from one place to another and then back again. In fact, that difference is a major way to distinguish between the two types.

A key to knowing how serious the pain is, is by it's location. If the pain is somewhere in the extremities, then the chances are, it's origin is musculoskeletal, in other words, more externally based. On the other hand, if the pain is in the torso, we must take it seriously because internal organs can be involved and the pain could be signaling a major imbalance. Of course, this is not always the case, but it's best to be cautious.

Pain or oppressive feelings in the chest for instance, should be dealt with immediately. Often it's best under these conditions to stop the exercise altogether and either sit or lie down until the feeling passes. That said, there can be rather intense or disquieting pains that come up temporarily and then disappear later in the standing session.

These are part of the body's natural healing process as severe or long term blockages try to open up. Bottom line, having a knowledgeable teacher is invaluable when it comes to the differentiation of pain and what to do or not do, about it.

**Dizziness and Nausea**

Where as it can sometimes be difficult to tell about pain, dizziness or nausea are definite red-flags. If either of these occur, cease practice and go sit or lie down and rest until the symptoms pass.

Dizziness is usually a sign of serious deficiency, such that the Upright Chi is failing to ascend to the head. But there are occasions when an excess condition is the cause, such as Liver wind or phlegm clouding or obstructing the orifices. These could be precursors to a heart attack or stroke. The important point is to take dizziness seriously.

Nausea, though uncomfortable is not usually as serious as dizziness. Nausea can be caused as simply as unknowingly having lifted or tensed the chest or abdomen during practice.

This reverses the direction of the Stomach Chi flow, which is naturally downward, and causes the Stomach Chi to rebel upwards, triggering nausea. Another cause can be internal tension linked to emotions.

**Emotional and Mental Anxiety**

After one has spent many years training Zhan Zhuang, they will have undergone both emotional and mental transformation. In order for this to happen, all the emotional baggage stored in the five Yin Organs will have had to have surfaced and been dissolved.

As part of this process many old and perhaps painful emotions will have come up, just as they were when the events happened. In essence, the temporary re-experiencing of these feelings is actually the way we cleanse and purify these blocked or negative emotions. Once these negative patterns have been dissolved, the quantity of vital energy previously bottled up is then recirculated back into our system as fresh, neutral energy. And this gives a tangible boost to our overall life-force.

The five Yin Organs and their corresponding emotions were listed earlier in The Transformation Process. In Taoism it is considered that both good virtue and negative virtue energies are stored in the organs and there is only so much 'storage space.' This means the more negative emotions we have collected, the less room there is for their good virtue counterparts. But that's a whole other story.

# WORKING WITH INJURIES

## WORKING WITH INJURIES

We all enter into the practice of Zhan Zhuang having sustained at least some sort of injury, even if it has apparently healed by itself. When injuries occur, especially anything fairly serious, the body goes into a balancing act and adapts. This means that new energetic and nerve patterns are created in the body's effort to heal itself.

What happens unfortunately, is that these patterns, which are supposed to be temporary modifications of the original matrix during the healing process, often become fixed. When this occurs, these temporary patterns become embedded in the subconscious and as such are no longer easily accessible through conscious manipulation.

This is the brilliance of the standing exercise, the ability to, over time, access these aberrant subconscious patterns and indeed correct them, meaning return them to their original matrix, prior to injury.

Of what do these patterns generally consist? For the sake of discussion, in terms of Zhan Zhuang and the internal martial arts, we will divide them into two categories. One is static (Zhan Zhuang) and the other is moving. (walking, Tai Chi, etc.) Of course, this is a bit arbitrary because elements of the static patterns can easily occur during movement.

On a postural level in Zhan Zhuang, we can apply the 'Weakest Link Model' to start breaking down the altered pattern in the injured area. Simply put, when entering into any posture, we allow the injured region or weakest link to dictate the amount of stretch that is appropriate. For example, let's say we have tightness or an injury somewhere in the Rhomboid muscles between the spine and the shoulder blades in the upper back. As we raise our arms up in say, the Holding the Ball posture, we first bring our feeling-awareness to the injured region and feel what is happening as we move our arms into position. If the area begins to get too tight or sore we must start again and reduce the size of the ball we're holding and also reduce the distance the elbow is, in front of the spine. When done right, there will be a gentle stretch to the injured area with no discomfort. This gentle stretching helps break up stagnation and increase local circulation. And since most long-standing injuries involve the local pooling and stagnation of Chi and blood which impede proper circulation, the Weakest Link Model can gradually reopen the affected region and help it heal.

The second category involves movement. These patterns are many times concerned with the firing of nerves in their correct sequence. Let's take walking for example. When we take a step, if the nerves are firing correctly, the weight of our body passes effortlessly through the left or right Chi Kung Channels (left or right sides of the body) until it reaches the bottom of our foot, where the process then reverses itself. This leads to what we would call a normal gait.

What happens when we're under the influence of an aberrated subconscious pattern is that there is a subtle, or in many cases, not so subtle misfiring of the nerves which appears to the observer as a glitch in the step or even a limp. The above is a simplified example and one of many aspects of the total procedure that must be dealt with, as anyone who has recovered from serious injury will tell you.

With these types of patterns we can use *Yiquan's* slow walking, both forward and *backward* to begin to correct the problem. The key with this is to move slow enough to where you can feel what is happening in the muscles as you take each step. That way, soon enough you will identify the problem area in the firing sequence. Once you have done this, the next step is to walk even a little slower in an effort to relax and reintegrate the suspect region. The trick to this is to avoid walking too slow. The problem with moving *too* slowly is that it will often create more tension, rather than relieving it. The best is the Golden Mean, not doing too much and not doing too little.

That said, there are a number of other factors which have to be reckoned with in order to effect a full recovery. Not the least of which is the energetic factor. It is this aspect that is almost completely overlooked in western physical-therapy but is in fact a most critical factor in that failing to properly address it, makes *complete* recovery generally impossible.

Let's see how the standing practice can be of assistance. By focusing our attention in the low Dan Tien or in the centerpoint between the navel and the *Ming Men*, we begin to access the body's energetic physical center and it's innate wisdom.

As my acupuncture mentor, one of the top doctors ever to leave China, used to say, "The body wants to heal itself." So the question becomes, how do we make contact with this power and eventually gain some control over it? There are two aspects to this. One is mental and the other, the most important, is through feeling.

The first part of this practice involves finding the energetic center of the body. Use the Finding Your Center method, to hone in on your centerpoint. At first this physical power center will be quite vague, but with daily practice you'll gradually begin to feel it more and more concretely. But what is it exactly that we should be feeling? Now this is where it gets interesting. At first, this sensation may manifest as any number of feelings. Depending on your previous background, you might get a feeling of warmth or coolness or wind or numbness or nothing at all, meaning nothing physically tangible. This process of focusing is similar to the kid's game of using the sun and a magnifying glass to make a piece of newspaper catch fire. The sun is the concentration of our intention - *Yi*. The magnifying glass is our relaxed one-pointed focus. The low Dan Tien or physical center of our body is the piece of newspaper. And the resulting fire is like the heat we feel after enough practice.

Of course this is just the beginning and the long term transformation process has many stages which will be discussed in more detail later. But for now, a simple understanding might go something like this. Once we can generate some warmth in our Dan Tien using the one-pointed focus of our *Yi* and feeling-awareness, two things usually happen. One, the warmth will increase in intensity sometimes getting quite hot before the Chi becomes abundant and overflows to the rest of the body. Many times this will make us sweat, often profusely. But later, with continued practice, this sensation will seem to mellow until one day, we no longer feel it in the same way because the frequency of the Chi has become the same temperature as our body. At that point, a certain conscious control over it's movement becomes possible.

The second thing that occurs is the feeling-development of our 'sense of center.' As stated earlier, at first this feeling is barely tangible but later it evolves into a palpable energetic reality. This speaks to the crystallization of the Chi and the development of the Golden Pearl.

All this is well and good but how can someone achieve this given only a limited sense of center? The answer lies in finding that energetic space in the center of your body (sometimes only a pinpoint) where there is no physical tension when you breathe. Even for a brand new learner this space already exists, even if at first it appears infinitesimally small. The truth is, this space already exists in every human being for if it did not, there would be no life because this energetic space is a basic link between the body and the life-sustaining and life-promoting Chi itself.

At this point we turn our attention to a most important concept and that is to grasp the difference between what the Chinese and the West think of as focus. In the case of western thought this implies a sense of tension, both mental and physical. (eyebrows scrunched, excessive concentration)

This is of course completely counterproductive and really has no place in the Chinese therapeutic exercises. (Zhan Zhuang, Tai Chi, Chi Kung) Instead, and this goes for breathing as well, we must cultivate a certain relaxed sense of focus which the Chinese call *Wu Wei* or doing without doing, mind of no-mind.

This means that after setting our intention, we find our center through feeling and dwell therein. We let go of conscious desire and from then on, focus in a relaxed manner.

This is akin to letting go of the desire for result, real or imagined, and simply holding our feeling-awareness in the chosen area almost as if we really didn't care.

In addition to the above, we must also take into consideration the important distinction between doing and *allowing*. Allowing is what 'doing without doing' implies. It is through allowing rather than doing that we achieve success with Zhan Zhuang.

In other words we must put aside our opinions, hopes and desires and investigate the nature of relaxation. For it is only through cultivating greater and greater relaxation over time that we eventually make contact with the subconscious after which, many wonderful things become possible including healing, self-defense power and higher energetic development.

So what does it really mean to relax. There are essentially three components, the physical aspect, the emotional aspect and the mental aspect. In truth, there is actually a fourth aspect which is the Shen or spirit but this subject would require an entire volume by itself. It has to do with such things as the karmic burden the individual brought into their present lifetime.

Although at first glance the physical aspect of relaxation appears self-evident, it still bears mentioning certain basic principals. For example, one may think they are adept at letting go of tension in the muscles but when they manually check certain locations, they still find tensions. What does this mean? The answer could lie in several areas such as the organs or how the emotions affect the physical body.

So let's say we can't fully release muscle tension in the lower back region. This could be due to an old injury, congestion and/or a blockage in the Kidneys. It's the same with the other organs and the physical regions in which they are located, as well as their meridians.

But there is another, perhaps even more important aspect and that is the emotions. In the case of the Kidneys, fear can effect the entire organism. In other words it has a systemic effect. So we must learn to differentiate between local tension and systemic tension.

Strong negative emotions can have a very deleterious effect on a person and that brings us to the powerful link between the emotions and the mind.

Certain thoughts trigger certain emotions which in turn generate tensions. We are consciously aware of some of these tensions, but not those still buried in the subconscious.

Therefore, it's easy to see that one's mental state will inevitably influence their daily practice. So a good place to start with gaining more relaxation is the calming of the mind and here is where the three basic aspects come full circle. By regulating our breath we gradually calm the mind which allows a deeper relaxation to penetrate our bodies. Also this regulating of the breath will concomitantly soothe and release emotions.

Perhaps now you can see how difficult it is to truly understand what the Chinese convey to one another in the two word phrase, *Wu Wei.*

With that in mind, let's revisit the basic Finding Your Center method, only this time using *Wu Wei* and pure *Nei Kung.*

This presupposes you've already completed the exercise using the physical 'hands' method. So now, to test your dimensional awareness, try removing your hands and returning them to the Wuji posture. Next, with feeling-awareness alone bring your attention to what you perceive as the front of your body, where your palm was touching, and then move it to the lower back, where the other hand was touching. Slowly toggle your attention back and forth between the front and back points, taking as much time as you need to actually gain a sense of feeling something tangible, even if that feeling is at first quite subtle.

In other words, use your mind to tell yourself this and only this is what you are going to do and then switch solely to your feeling-awareness and slowly toggle it.

As we get better and better at feeling instead of thinking, eventually the mind will quiet and we will find ourselves dwelling in the realm of pure feeling which is our doorway into the subconscious.

Having achieved the above, continued daily practice will eventually yield the ability to gain an understanding of the subconscious and inevitably communicate and influence it. This understanding will not be so much mental, but rather through feeling and direct perception. Of course at the beginning, the ability to stay with the pure feeling state is quite transient and no sooner do we feel something unusual, than our mind cuts in and tries to analyze it. When this happens, don't be discouraged, simply refocus and reenter the pure feeling realm.

Although there will be an initial struggle between these two elements (mind and feeling) after enough training, the mind will submit to spirit and become more quiescent.

This marks the point where transcendent experiences can begin to happen. One of the first of these is what I call a 'time warp,' You think you've been standing fifteen minutes or so, but have in fact stood for nearly an hour. *Wang Xiang Zhai* called this dwelling in the Void.

Another manifestation is the sudden acquisition of knowledge or awareness, like the ability to perform certain martial applications that were previously unknown or impossible for you.

All this and much more happens when one day the Chi passes freely through the Central Channel, comes out the top of the head and then recycles itself like a warm rain falling down.

## MUSCLE BLOCKAGES AND RELEASING THEM

When we have a muscular injury, in most cases the muscle contracts like a spring, upward and inward. If this is not resolved, then ultimately the injured muscle becomes 'stuck' to the bone, fascia or other nearby muscles.

When this happens the pain or discomfort becomes pretty much constant. To resolve this type of injury, we primarily use the descending, lengthening Heaven energy.

In extreme cases however, it is also possible for the opposite to happen. The muscle 'spring' can be so sprung that flaccidity occurs.

This can be particularly challenging when tendons and ligaments are involved. In this case, in addition to the descending Heaven energy, we must rely heavily on the rising, lifting Earth energy to slowly retighten the spring.

The good news is, with time, Zhan Zhuang can resolve and heal many of these injuries. What actually happens is that the contracted muscle elongates and becomes unstuck from the bone.

This process can sometimes be quite strenuous, especially when long unused/newly freed muscles come back online or when the body attempts to return to the original energy flows that were present before injury.

But if one is persistent, with continued daily practice, these sinews gradually regain their elasticity, strength and correct dynamic tension, and the soreness vanishes. Please note: If the injury is severe, this process can take a long time.

The key to consciously releasing blockages is the use of what I'll call 'The Horizontal and Vertical Matrix.' The idea is simple. Muscle and sinew problems generally result in a contraction of some sort.

Sometimes this contraction can be vertical. For example, the attachments of the muscles of the upper arm are all jammed up into the shoulder. Other times the contraction can be horizontal, like pain caused by the Piriformis muscle in the hip and buttocks. Or it can be a combination of both.

Once we know where the problem is, we focus on the location. It often helps to physically touch the area to bring it to the attention of the conscious mind.

After that, focus just above the blockage and relax the tissue down through the suspect area and from there on down to clearly below it. This should cause the tightness to ease up, at least a little. Eventually, after much experience, a release like this in the head, neck or torso will percolate all the way down to the feet.

Once you've gained a little release in the vertical direction, it often helps to coordinate with the breath, especially the inhale. When we exhale, accept for reverse breath, the body's sinews tend to condense or contract.

On the other hand, when we inhale normally, things tend to inflate and expand. It's this expansion that we're looking for. The idea is to make space in the previously congested area.

*The trick to this is learning how to physically let go while inhaling and expanding*. This is where the mind comes into play. We use the mind to 'see' and feel the specific area and surrounding vicinity. We want to feel like the tissues are surrendering to gravity and literally letting go, the muscles 'falling' and lengthening.

Imagine a small rock attached to a string. Now, while holding the end of the string in one hand and the rock in the other, let go of the rock. The feeling is sort of like that.

Now, the horizontal method is basically the same as the vertical, except we're letting go laterally. In order to execute this properly, we first do the vertical release from above and as soon as we feel some movement there, we apply the horizontal release which should percolate toward the sides of the torso or the outsides of the arm or leg.

In addition to these methods which tend to feel fairly linear, there is a three-dimensional release which stems from the application of the Vertical and Horizontal methods plus the final dimension of depth.

This is essentially Spherical Opening. The idea is to find the dead center of the pain or problem and imagine it as an extremely small sphere. Next, relax and release outwardly in all directions as if the tiny sphere was expanding to fill the whole area.

When you can get this one to work, you feel like you've created more space in your body. This is sometimes known as creating emptiness.

Lastly, there may be some circumstances where this doesn't seem to work, at least very well. When this happens, it generally means a large region surrounding the problem location is also affected.

If such is the case, you might want to physically stretch the whole area. Let's say the problem is in the middle back. We'll use a variation of Sitting on a High Stool to help open the body.

1) Assume the Wuji posture.

2) Inhale and raise your hands high over your head for a moment, stretching the torso upwards.

3) Next, while keeping the feeling of the torso in it's expanded state, exhale and lower your arms. Now try the Spherical method again.

Nearly all muscle and sinew injuries require the use of the descending Heaven energy, but some very serious traumas which result in an overextension of muscles, tendons or ligaments, leading to a degree of flaccidity or lack of tensile strength, require the extensive participation of the rising Earth energy as well. Let's take a blockage in the thigh as our example.

Once the Heaven energy has descended from the Kua through the thigh and into the knee and foot, there is a degree of muscular elongation. This elongation may mostly be in the front thigh muscles however. In that case, the rising, Earth energy will help lift and open the hamstrings so that the length of the front and back elongations will feel more or less the same. When there is an equal amount of both the descending and ascending energies coursing freely through a region, we say that region has become open and balanced.

However, if flaccidity or general weakness has occurred, in its effort to lift and lengthen, the Earth energy may not pass freely upward in which case various 'shakings' will occur as the rising energy slowly restores tensile strength to the muscle fibers, tendons or ligaments.

## THE DANGER OF OVER-ADJUSTING POSTURES

When we have a blockage, that is, discomfort or pain, the tendency is to try to adjust and relieve it. The danger with this is that *it's easy to overcorrect or misjudge the problem.*

Excessive movement and or misalignment can cause a war between the various dynamic tensions inside the body at that location. By this I mean, the Heaven and Earth energies strain and fight one another for control of the blocked area.

At the beginning, the biggest problem we have with releasing blockages is to ascertain the exact center of the problem. This lack of feeling is often due to diminished body consciousness.

This often happens with long term problems or severe damage. The brain simply turns off or greatly lessens the feeling in the particular region.

To get around this, we can use techniques like the Station Method. Another way is to use micro-movements to make even more subtle adjustments. When one has achieved a certain level, then just by putting their inner sight and feeling-awareness in a specific part of the body, they are able to influence and make changes in muscular relaxation.

These changes will not be visible to the untrained observer. But if the observer were to place their hand on the affected muscles, they would certainly *feel* the change.

This is one of the primary differences between the external and internal martial arts. In the external systems, the muscular changes are deliberately overt and clearly differentiated. On the other hand, with the internal system, the greater the achievement, the less visible it becomes. The reason for this is, at advanced levels, the changes are primarily occurring deep inside the body or in the energy body, which then influences the physical.

So as you can see, there are basically two ways of adjusting postures, an external visible manner and an internal, not so visible manner.

When one has reached a modicum of achievement, they can then assume a posture, position the limbs in perfect symmetry and feel where the odd or uncomfortable regions are. At that point, one uses their inner sight and feeling-awareness to make the relaxation adjustments.

This is one of the reasons why the ability to make changes in the body, purely with the mind and feeling, is so highly prized.

Another reason is that in martial arts, this same ability is used to control the opponent at contact and issue power with little or no visibility, in other words, non-telegraphically. This is one of the reasons why very high level internal martial artists are usually superior to their external style counterparts.

Now, this is all well and good if you've got 15 or 20 years experience, but what if you don't? As explained before, for those starting out, often the most difficult task is to pinpoint the real source of the problem.

The difficulty is, at the beginning, our whole-body awareness is minimal. *We think the problem's in one location but the source is actually elsewhere.*

The same is often true in the Tai Chi form movements. At home we feel like were doing it correctly, but when we take a lesson, the teacher makes many corrections and we realize we were not. The good news is that our body-awareness grows every time we train Zhan Zhuang.

One method to help improve our feeling ability is to actually touch the specific location if possible, otherwise have a partner or spouse do it. For this example, we'll use some place you can reach yourself, the Deltoid.

**Touching To Memorize Feeling**

1) Assume the Holding the Ball posture.

2) Now, while keeping the left arm in place, put your right palm and fingers on the Deltoid and where it connects to the shoulder.

3) Then, while holding that light touch, exhale first and then inhale and relax the area, letting it surrender to gravity. If done right, you'll feel some elongation and relaxation in the muscles you're touching.

4) Now that you have a *concrete* feeling of the location, return the right arm to it's original position and try again. Remember the feeling where the palm was touching, then use the breath as indicated above. You should be able to feel some release just with breath, mind and feeling. Don't be surprised if adjacent areas also try to elongate and let go. If that happens, you're definitely on the right track. So to avoid over-adjusting postures, apply the following principals.

1) *Know* the epicenter of the discomfort.
2) Try using only the mind and feeling-awareness first.
3) Use micro-movements without altering overall structure.
4) Know when to resist making changes and just wait it out.

## USING GRAVITY TO RELEASE PRESSURES

The Station Method is a good example of using gravity to equalize and balance the Chi and body pressures. By relaxing the station above the problem, we allow gravity to help open the tissue.

The idea of Chi pressure and the way it functions in the body bears taking a look at. Think of the Chi pressure in the body like the air in an inflated tire. If the tire pressure isn't correct, the vehicle doesn't ride right.

Too little Chi pressure is like an under-inflated tire. Too little pressure creates deficiency in organs and other body systems. To understand the reason for this, for a moment think of the meridians as tubes with water flowing through them. Without enough 'water' pressure the body's systems don't have enough energy and therefore do not function optimally.

On the other end of the spectrum, we have the over-inflated tire or the excess condition of too much Chi pressure. The problems this can cause are quite evident. Too much pressure in the Heart will lead to high Bp numbers and risk of heart attack or stroke. Too much arterial pressure and the effected region could burst.

Those are extreme examples. Usually with the more moderate Excess conditions, there are feelings of local or systemic tightness and often times people unknowingly manifest this tension in there daily lives.

Once again, if the tightness, stiffness or uncomfortable pressure is somewhere in the torso we must always be on the lookout for possible organ problems especially if there are corresponding symptoms.

That said, we can use specific breathing patterns to help equalize imbalances in Chi pressure. The idea is simple, for deficient Chi pressure, inhale longer than you exhale. For an excess condition, simply exhale longer than you inhale in your breathing cycle.

Gravity, such as it is on Earth, is an irresistible force, which over time takes its toll on the body. Witness the sagging of certain regions and many times the actual contraction of the spine and a shrinkage in height.

Thank goodness gravity or the descending Heaven energy is balanced by an equal and opposite force, the rising Earth energy or ascending Earth Chi.

For those of later years, as long as you're still walking around, you've got at least some rising Earth Chi which with the help of Zhan Zhuang can be cultivated, nurtured and strengthened. This revivified Earth Chi then acts as a powerful counterbalance to many of gravity's effects which we call aging.

So the question becomes, how can we access this powerful anti-aging force. Like so many things in the internal arts, the answer appears to be a bit of a paradox.

First let me add that every time you take a step and you feel your weight move through the *Yongquan* point of the foot as you move forward, there is the rising Earth Chi.

This explains one of the reasons that walking is such an effective exercise. Here of course, I'm speaking of conscious or focused walking. And since we're talking about walking I would like to emphasize the great efficacy of backward walking.

In today's society most people are on the go and in a hurry. You can see this in the way they walk, everything juts out and seems to almost push forward. This leading with the chest or in boxing they would say, leading with the chin, takes it's toll physically both on the internal organs and the body's structural balance, actually deforming it. Backward walking can help correct some of these effects by literally reversing the directions of the movements.

Here is the idea of paradox. By doing the opposite of what you might think, you achieve results. With walking, its doing it backwards. With a body that's become a victim of gravity, we use the opposite, the Earth's rising energy to augment, counterbalance and stave off possible future effects. This effort is well worth the time if you step back and look at the big picture.

So, remember that we are constantly activating the rising Earth Chi every time we walk, either forward or backwards. This is also true with standing, but there the mechanism is somewhat different.

Because we're standing still, the imprint of gravity tends to feel greater than when we're moving. This has to do with momentum and the laws of physics. 'A body at rest tends to stay at rest and a body in motion tends to stay in motion.'

This means that during our stand, we must find a way to overcome the force of gravity and access the ascending Earth Chi in order to bolster our Upright Chi.

Now here's that paradox again. In order to gain the utility of the rising Earth Chi, we must first work with the opposite, that is, take advantage of gravity and use it to sink the Chi below our feet, at which point, the rising Earth energy seems to open and become active of itself.

# METHOD TO RELEASE UNKNOWN BLOCKAGES

Sometimes, no matter how skilled and perceptive we are, we just can't get some area in the body to let go and open up. When this occurs, try using *Wang Xiang Zhai's* method for resolving difficult blockages.

**Wang's Method**

1) Assume the Wuji posture, then close your jaw and lightly clench your teeth.

2) Press the tongue firmly to the roof of your mouth, while keeping the jaw muscles relaxed enough to feel that the upper and lower teeth are still touching.

Since an enormous amount of tension is often stored in the jaw, pay particular attention to the upper and lower Masseter muscles and the Stomach points *Xiaguan* ST-7 and *Jiache* ST-6.

3) Next, open your wrist and ankle joints.

These two locations play an important energetic role in the body's proper functioning. One of the reasons for this is that the Transport points of the Stomach, Liver and Spleen are located at the ankles. Transport points facilitate the smooth movement of the Chi.

The wrists are also significant in that they are the home of the powerful Source points of the Lung, Pericardium and Heart. In addition, *Taiyuan* LU-9, the Lung Source point, is also its Transport point and the all-important 'Meeting Point of the Blood Vessels' for the entire body. By opening this location, we are able to improve the efficiency of the blood and *Ying Chi* (Nutritive Chi) flow, throughout the vascular system. Also, the significance of abundant *Kong Chi* and increased blood flow through more open and elastic arteries and veins cannot be overestimated. So much of our proper systemic daily function is clearly dependent on them. It is by achieving this heightened state that we provide the extra energy necessary to clear blockages and restore Chi and blood flow. By getting the flow going, we prepare the body for the subconscious instructions it is about to receive in the next phase.

4) Finally, place your attention on *Feng Fu* point GV-16 at the base of the skull and just feel. This point is also known as *Yu Jen*, the Jade Pillow in Taoism. No matter what seems to be happening in the body, for this method to work you must keep your attention at the base of the skull, but there is a catch. This brings us to the use of our peripheral awareness.

While the majority of our feeling-awareness and focus is at the base of the skull, we use our peripheral kinesthetic awareness to become cognizant of the whole while we feel the workings of the body, changing, adapting, opening, adjusting and condensing in order to come into a more integrated, interconnected and unified balance.

This method is a perfect example of relying on the body's innate wisdom and ability to heal itself in that we are focusing on the location where all nerve messages from the brain pass through to the body and vice-versa. In addition, *Feng Fu* point has a strong relationship with the sacral region through what's called the Sacral and Cranial pumps, the mechanisms that move cerebrospinal fluid up the spinal column.

Of course, Wang's method is an advanced technique, primarily because of the necessity to open parts of the body at will and also the ability to utilize multiple feeling-awareness.

## WORKING WITH ENERGETIC DYNAMIC TENSIONS

One of the first things we encounter energetically in our standing meditation, is the balance that is trying to occur between the descending Heaven energy (gravity) and the ascending Earth energy, which is the basis and support of our Upright Chi, that is, our ability to stand, walk around and function normally as human beings.

We've already spoken of the need to use the descending energy first and only when the Chi sinks beneath our feet, does the rising Earth energy come into play. Of course, there will be individual locations in the body that call out for the lifting energy straightaway. In these instances, it is only common sense that we make the local adjustments that particular region of the body is asking for.

That said, there is an important reason for the order first implied, that is, using the descending energy first and then only after that, bringing in the ascending, lifting energy.

The reason has to do with grounding. Many eastern paths concentrate exclusively on the rising Earth energy to lead them to enlightenment, Kundalini Yoga for example.

The problem with this is that when something extraordinary does happen, the excess energy is often not grounded, meaning it has no root and as a result, too much of the energy sticks in the head, resulting in mental and emotional imbalances, often times severe.

This stems from the fact that the powerful rising force has been unable to properly exit the body through *Baihui* point or the Crown chakra or, that some of the other psychic centers did not adequately open. As a result, this often overwhelming energy has no place to vent and becomes stuck in the head or other potentially dangerous areas in the body. These changes are often instantaneous and can include major metabolic shifts as well. This is where the wisdom of the Taoists comes in. By first opening and clearing the body from the top down, we create a connection with the Earth which acts as a safety-valve when the powerful ascending energies do open up.

If the aspirant's consciousness is advanced enough, the volcanic rising energy exits the body through the top of the head and the problem is solved, meaning this is the natural outcome and the excess energy is balanced and/or vented off in the person's larger energy-field.

But even if not, for one who has first worked with Zhan Zhuang and the descending energy, certain safe passages, vents or outlets will kick in to prevent a dangerous amount of excess energy from remaining lodged in the head, chest or abdomen.

But before all this fantastic stuff can take place, the balancing of the Heaven and Earth energies will have already created at least a relative degree of whole body integration and unification. This will have largely been the result of the hardwiring process, both physically and energetically.

This creation of an open vessel itself, heals and strengthens the body and prepares it for the day when the energy rises and we safely receive small portions of 'enlightenment.'

The truth is, it's only when the body has become unified physically, that working with the more purely energetic states becomes viable and effective. I once asked a famous teacher, "What is the ultimate state of Zhan Zhuang and Tai Chi?" And the reply was, "Sphericality...be like a single cell or big ball, both in stillness and in movement."

# THE TRANSFORMATION PROCESS REVISITED

## THE TRANSFORMATION PROCESS REVISITED

What is actually happening physically and energetically when we stand? What are the roles of the skin, the muscles, tendons, ligaments and bones.

Then on a deeper level, what is happening to the organs, glands, bone marrow, the Chi and finally the emotions, mind, and spirit of the practitioner? These are the sixty-four billion dollar questions.

The overall transformation process is very much like a complex jigsaw puzzle. Back in the day, kids were often given beautiful puzzles with hundreds of pieces. And just as with these puzzles, the end result of Zhan Zhuang is something truly amazing.

But there's just one thing. The puzzle of the human body is not two dimensional, but three. Actually it's multi-dimensional when we consider the subtle bodies, not to mention the emotions and the mind.

Assembling these old-fashioned puzzles very much mirrors what happens to the body/mind/spirit on it's way to Unity. Each piece must first be found and it's place in the puzzle located.

Each has its particular position and must fit in correctly with all the surrounding pieces. And as the puzzle starts to be more assembled, all of a sudden we recognize larger images and structure.

So it is with the body. As larger areas of the body, big sections and groups of muscles for example, open up and become linked energetically, there is often a geometric leap in relaxation and/or awareness due to the enhanced Chi flow, stemming from the greater connectivity. This is a large part of the physical transformation.

When all the pieces of the puzzle have been discovered and assigned their proper place, (whole body integration) we finally have, pardon the expression, the whole picture. So we will begin with the outside of the body and progress inward.

**Skin**

The skin is our outermost connection to the 'external' world, the air around us, the warmth of the sun above us and the feel of the Earth beneath our feet. When we stand, the pores of our skin open and eventually pulse with our breath. This opening more deeply connects us with our immediate environment. The transformation of the skin is reflected in an increase in its softness and elasticity. This happens because of the increased Chi flow and greater oxygenation of the blood as our pores pulse open and closed. In addition to expelling toxins or toxic Chi, opening of the pores also allows us to also absorb rejuvenating external, environmental Chi into the outer layers of the skin.

**Muscles**

The muscles act as our balance and support in congress with the tendons, ligaments and bones. Transformation involves, repairing, strengthening, balancing, elongation and the cultivation of a soft spring-like effect which makes standing feel like *Wu Wei*. And with that, comes the finer and finer refinement of balance.

Elongation is also reflected in the development of a connected strength, like you see in the body of a championship swimmer. Also the development of the springy strength, helps the muscles become more defined. One of my teachers looked like he lifted free-weights for years, when in fact he only trained Zhan Zhuang and Tai Chi. As regards health, extended Zhan Zhuang practice can actually heal and repair many types of damaged muscle tissue, including certain kinds of tears. It seems the enhanced Chi flow creates an energetic bridge between the torn fibers, which eventually fills in with physical tissue.

**Sinews**

The tendons and ligaments naturally function in conjunction with the muscles, especially during movement. One of the main differences between the two is the amount of voltage or juice they are able to transmit. Think of the body as an electrical grid. We'll consider the *Shen*, Heart, Brain, Bone Marrow, and Central Channel/low Dan Tien as the main power station. Using that analogy, the sinews are the substations and the muscles are the lines to the residential areas.

The sinews, therefore, are capable of conducting far stronger amounts of bio-electromagnetic energy than are the muscles by themselves. This explains why, as one becomes more advanced in their ability to issue Fa Jing power, more and more of their charge is transmitted through the sinews, bones and the three *Chi Kung* Channels, rather than relying so much on the muscles, as is common at earlier stages. Of course, the tendons and ligaments also play an important role in the refinement of balance, as well as being a salient factor in the springiness of the joints. One of the reasons this powerful spring-like energy manifests, is due to the continuous pulsing of all the joints in the body that occurs after enough Zhan Zhuang training.

**Bones**

The bones are our foundation. When, after much practice the muscles and sinews have opened, we find ourselves essentially balancing on the alignment of our bone structure. When the Chi is regularly permeating the body during one's standing sessions, it begins to penetrate the bones and starts to rejuvenate and revitalize the bone marrow. This is so important because the bone marrow is responsible for among other things, the template from which our red blood cells are created. So this is one of the ways Zhan Zhuang can lead to the healing of many health problems and the possibility of what the Taoist's call radiant health. Energetically, the bones are also powerful conductors of bio-electromagnetic energy and electricity itself. This is what scientists call the Piezoelectric polarization effect. The increased Chi flow and bio-electromagnetic energy conducted through the bones, during Zhan Zhuang practice, has the effect of creating *greater bone density*. This is of vital importance as we grow older.

**Organs**

The internal organs are the storehouse of profound energies, critically important to the health and proper functioning of the entire organism. While this is fairly obvious, the connection to the subtle bodies, especially in regard to the emotions, effects our entire being.

As the Chi becomes abundant and overflows, the process of tonification (of Deficient conditions) and the reduction (of Excess conditions) takes place in the organs, as it does energetically, with all the aspects of the physical body. Whereas muscles contain cellular memory, the organs are the home of deep-seated emotions and emotional patterns. As cleansing and repair occur, the toxic energy and negative emotions surface to be expunged. This surfacing is an opportunity, not a guarantee. To put it simply, some people are better at letting go and releasing their past than others.

**Emotions**

This element of Zhan Zhuang's transformational ability is one of the most important in that it directly impacts our daily lives and personal interactions. There are a number of sources on the web which point out the various correspondences between particular organs and the emotions they house. But it is the ability to neutralize and transform our negative emotional content, at which Zhan Zhuang really excels.

Take patience for example and it's evil twin, impatience. Traditionally these emotions are linked to the Heart energy. But really when you think about it, the whole proposition of standing in one place for a fair amount of time, requires a certain amount of patience to begin with. On a deeper level, when the Heart Chi is in balance, this reflects outwardly as a calmer person, at ease with themselves.

There is one final element concerning Zhan Zhuang and the emotions. This is the long term effect our feeling-awareness has when focused in any of the three Dan Tiens, but especially inside the low Dan Tien.

In addition to the effect the Chi has on each of the individual organs, over time a gathering and unification takes place in the low Dan Tien. This gathering mixes many types of the body's Chi, including some from each organ into a big 'energy stew,' which is then 'cooked' by our continued focus. This 'cooking' further purges and purifies the emotions to the point of neutrality, at which time this newly-refined energy is returned to the organs, often greatly enhancing their function.

**Glands**

The glands come into play, beyond their normal functions, in alchemy and meditation. When we do Zhan Zhuang, as part of the overall organism, the glands are naturally affected. It is important to note here that although they all have different functions, there is an internal linkage which makes each gland aware of and responsive to all of the others.

The glands can also effect metabolism. Those with metabolic issues often find that Zhan Zhuang training helps rebalance and regulate elements of this mechanism. It does this through the increased Chi flow which augments or reduces as necessary. The Chi, just like the body has an innate intelligence with which it functions.

**Chi**

The Chi is the all important factor that makes transformation possible in the first place. One example of this is our immune system. After much practice, as the *Ying* (nutritive) Chi becomes abundant and the internal organs are saturated, the extra will be stored in the fascia and beneath the skin where its abundance strengthens the *Wei Chi*.

The *Wei Chi* is the Chi which generally resides in the area from just beyond the skin through the first few layers of the epidermis, dermis and eventually the subcutaneous tissue as well. This is in a sense the western equivalent of our immune system's first line of defense. Think of it as something like an outdoor bug-light. As the insects approach, they are zapped. This is what happens all the time when this part of our immune system is functioning correctly.

An example of super-abundant *Wei Chi* are the *Chi Kung* demos where bare-chested people are poked with sharp weapons and are not cut and do not bleed. Part of this is the very real *Nei Kung* ability to shut down the blood flow in certain areas.

One of my teachers could pierce the soft tissue at the front of the throat with a bicycle spoke and then hook a rope over it and pull a jeep, a big military one. Then he'd remove the bicycle spoke and there would be no blood. Of course this requires inordinate skill in mobilizing and controlling the Chi.

So what happens is, as our Chi becomes truly abundant, the strength of this electromagnetic charge is greatly increased and one result is that the colds and flu which knock others down, don't seem to effect us.

All this comes about by first being able to 'sink the Chi.' This is a phrase we here often, but what does it really mean? Like much in the internal arts, there's a bit of a paradox to it or a dichotomy at the very least. While there is a real solid feeling of linkage and connection with the Earth, at the same time there is a lightness or emptiness throughout the body and also a springiness. Another way of thinking about it is as the ultimate adaptive state. Relaxed and calm, yet capable of instantaneous and powerful action.

Another aspect of sinking the Chi is the element of unified movement. "One part moves, all parts move..." This unified or spherical movement incorporates many of the laws of physics, only applied energetically to great result.

**Mind**

The mind plays a most critical role in the entire process. The aspect of mental discipline required to maintain the proper one-pointed internal focus, refines the various aspects of the mind and puts them under our control. This refining of the mind is a requisite achievement before one can be successful at the various advanced *Nei Kung* practices, the Fire method, the Water method, etc.

Also there is an overall effect on the mind and mental processes from the healing and purification of the organs, glands and the body's tissues. Much of this is due to the two-way link between the emotions and thought. As emotions are released, the mind calms and as the mind calms the emotions settle.

As one of my teachers once said, "When the Chi reaches the brain, you just get smarter." But its not just intelligence that's affected it's also one's *awareness*. This alone can have a life-changing effect on the practitioner.

## THE PARADOX OF INTERNAL POWER

Regarding internal power, one of my teachers once told me, "The stronger you feel, the weaker you are, and the weaker you feel, the stronger you are."

On the one hand, this means when you feel like you really hit hard, your internal power is actually weak. Conversely, when you feel like you really didn't do that much in terms of force, your internal power is actually abundant. And to take that a step further, when you feel like you 'didn't do anything,' other than execute the movement cleanly and effortlessly, that's often when you really issued a blast.

This has to do with the Chi permeating every fiber of your being and when it does, it creates a state of very contained potential energy, bubbling deep within, you might say.

So the feeling of muscular strength is replaced with a feeling of extreme lightness, (emptiness) speed and *intention*, like you can move your body as fast as your mind. As you might imagine, this is particularly useful in a real time self-defense situation.

This lightness, meaning the feeling of having no weight or resistance to movement from the environment, (the air) can permeate the body all the way down through the feet which become filled with spring power.

I once observed a master practitioner who could actually create a sort of temporary vacuum within which to move and strike.

Another manifestation of correctly channeled adrenalin is that everything above the level of our centerpoint (navel area) becomes extremely light (empty) while the sinking Chi makes everything in the lower half of the body filled with spring power, the ability to move in any direction instantaneously. Of course this division can be instantly modified, blended or reversed as the situation requires.

The activation of this 'readiness state' has to do with the role of adrenalin in a real-life situation and the difference between the way it acts on the trained or untrained person. In the untrained, the speed up of the heart rate and metabolism generate an overwhelming tension because instead of sinking, the Chi rises, usually into the chest and head.

In the highly trained individual however, the Chi sinks just as it always does after decades of *Wuji Kung Fu.* (Zhan Zhuang) This means that the energy reacts in such a way that all our resources are instantly mustered and ready for use.

To take all this a step further, we must discover the difference between the way physical power feels and the way that genuine internal power really feels.

The easiest place to start is to think of internal power as something not ruled by physicality. In other words, if in your mind, inside yourself, you can gather a volcanic explosive force and issue it instantaneously at the speed of thought, this does not have very much dependence on the physical delivery, which chances are will be smooth and internally explosive on contact.

But here's where people get off track. They think that speed and explosiveness are all there is to internal power. These two factors are the delivery method, nothing more. The content, the Chi or bio-electromagnetic energy actually does not respond well to tension, in fact tension cuts off or short-circuits Chi flow.

But when one gets good, I mean *really* good, even the speed and explosiveness necessary to create a dramatic reaction in the target, will seem to diminish or actually disappear.

In other words, the movement may appear very small, slow and smooth but the opponent's reaction will be anything but.

Upon seeing this for the first time, the mind has a little trouble putting it all together because the appearance of what happens seems to defy logic. How can a small, soft, short movement create such a sharp and violent reaction in the recipient?

The answer is of course, the Chi, or more correctly very condensed or crystallized Chi on the Yang side (electric) combining with the ethereal, less tangible *Yin Chi* (magnetic) to create a momentary electromagnetic charge or field. If this charge is strong enough it can disrupt or displace the recipient's field, causing instantaneous and chaotic reactions.

With a few very advanced practitioners, this can be like the feeling of sticking your finger in a light socket. *Chen Fa Ke* comes to mind in this regard.

So, the paradox of internal power seems to be; by releasing the need for physical speed and power as a source of strength, we unlock the door to an internal strength that inevitably has almost no limitation.

## PERSONALITY CHANGE

As a result of the many factors already mentioned, after decades of training one's consciousness tends to expand and generally soften. This means that as a result of all your practice, much of your physical problems (physical karma) has generally been resolved.

It also means in terms of your organs most of the stored negative-virtue-emotion and painful cellular memories have been largely discharged and neutralized, allowing almost a clean slate.

This probably means little to someone in their twenties or thirties but for those getting on in years it is a magic touchstone. Health as we age is perhaps the most prized possession.

Clearing out and healing the past, leads to dwelling more and more in the present. And it is in the present moment that all genuine achievements are wrought.

There are other types of personality change which are far more sinister. We see these portrayed in Hong Kong Kung Fu movies where two students study under the same master, but then one goes bad.

This means instead of allowing the training to change and evolve consciousness, an egomaniac or incredibly selfish or bitter person resists the change, and seeks to control it instead. Of course this creates a full blown sociopath, who inevitably must be put down.

Another aspect of personality change, is the profound increase in one's perception and a radical increase in sensitivity to all manner of energies.

Eventually it becomes easy to read a person's real intent or state of mind. In the same vein, people's true emotions become like an open book. This ability can be developed to the point where it actually borders on telepathy.

In addition, this skill is useful in both social situations as well as dubious, possibly dangerous environments.

The idea of increased perception covers so many areas. These might include greater awareness of what's actually going on in one's body or greater awareness of what's going on in one's environment. This can include persons and animals as well.

But by far, Zhan Zhuang's finest achievement is a greater perception of life, what it means, it's potentialities, it's possibilities, and then there's the expansion of our precious imagination, which sows the seeds for our future and beyond. With our imagination unleashed, there is virtually no limit to what we can do.

# EXPLORING THE HIGHER LEVELS

## THE BEST TIMES TO STAND

In a sense, anytime is a good time to practice your standing meditation. That said, there are four times that have special significance.

**Sunrise**
15 minutes before through 15 minutes after sunrise. This is when the Yin of night is changing into the Yang of day. Yin changing into Yang.

**Sunset**
15 minutes before through 15 minutes after sunset. This is the time during which the Yang energy of day changes into the Yin energy of night. Yang changing into Yin.

**High Noon**
The next time is 12 noon. This is the time when the Yang energy of day is ascendant and most abundant. In other words, this is the time of day when the greatest amount of Yang Chi is available.

**Midnight**
The last of the four special times is 12 midnight, the time of pure Yin, where the Yin energy is in it's greatest abundance. Training at this time can also be linked to the Yin energy of the moon.

When this method is used, the moon energy is drawn in through *Huiyin* point CV-1, the confluence of Yin, in the Perineum at the bottom of the torso, rather than through the *Baihui* point GV-20, the confluence of Yang at the top of the head.

This Yin moon energy generally has a perceptible coolness to it in contrast to the Yang energy, which feels warm. Night energy in general is cool, while daylight energy tends to be warm.

If one has a problem as termed in Chinese Medicine, deficient Yang, it then behooves them to do their practice at around 12 noon. At this time, it becomes possible to generate and encourage more Yang energy.

On the other hand, if your problem is deficient Yin, then great efficacy can be found by practicing at midnight.

During these Yang and Yin specific practice times we can also make use of the *Jing Luo*, the Channels and Collaterals, in other words we can work with the various meridians to bring about a better balanced state in the body. This also includes using the two hour organ circulation cycles. A detailed breakdown of the organ Chi circulation times is listed a little later.

So, say for example, we have lung difficulties. Then, if we're awake between 3am and 5am, we can move energy through the vectors of the Lung meridian, from its origin point in the corner of the chest to its end point near the thumb nail. The additional Lung Chi available at this time can do wonders in opening up passages and improving respiration. This is an excellent adjunct for people with Asthma.

Now a word on the time 15 minutes before, through 15 minutes after sunrise. When we have been sick or we are weak or just old, one of the first things to go is termed in Chinese Medicine, the *Yangming* energy, the Yang brightness energy. This could be considered that sparkle we have, something everyone has felt at certain times throughout their life.

So, working in the early morning between 5:00am and 7:00am, the time of the Yangming or Large Intestine circulation, can help to restore and rejuvenate some of this energy that is so easily lost through the various factors already mentioned.

It is often the case that one will feel quite cool outdoors when the session first begins. But by the time it's over, the body will have acclimatized and actually feel warm on the inside and cool on the outside. This can be termed, 'hot and cold positive,' and is an excellent sign. When I practice at this time, I never fail to become enriched and expanded throughout the rest of my day. So from my point of view, this is absolutely the best time to practice if possible. It can give a whole sparkle to the start of your day and energize your body.

Next, we will examine the Chi circulation times of the organs. Practicing Zhan Zhuang at these particular times can greatly augment the Chi of the individual organs.

**List of Organ Chi Circulation Times**

| Time | Element | Organ | Type of Chi |
|---|---|---|---|
| 5:00am - 7:00am | Metal | Large Intestine | Arm Yangming |
| 7:00am - 9:00am | Earth | Stomach | Foot Yangming |
| 9:00am -11:00am | Earth | Spleen | Foot Taiyin |
| 11:00am - 1:00pm | Fire | Heart | Arm Shaoyin |
| 1:00pm - 3:00pm | Fire | Small Intestine | Arm Taiyang |
| 3:00pm - 5:00pm | Water | Urinary Bladder | Foot Taiyang |
| 5:00pm - 7:00pm | Water | Kidneys | Foot Shaoyin |
| 7:00pm - 9:00pm | Ministerial Fire | Pericardium | Arm Jueyin |

| Time | Element | Organ | Type of Chi |
|---|---|---|---|
| 9:00pm - 11:00pm | Ministerial Fire | Triple Burner | Arm Shaoyang |
| 11:00pm - 1:00am | Wood | Gall Bladder | Foot Shaoyang |
| 1:00am - 3:00am | Wood | Liver | Leg Jueyin |
| 3:00am - 5:00am | Metal | Lungs | Arm Taiyin |

During each two hour period, the particular organ system has more energy available to it than the other twenty two hours of the daily cycle. Please note: A stand during the times listed above, can be used for both Excess and Deficient organ conditions. So, if one is suffering from an organ deficiency, practicing during that organ's abundant period can help nurture and augment it's Chi. If one's problem is excess, practicing during the particular organ's circulation time provides an opportunity to safely vent its excess Chi.

It's interesting to note the relationship between each of the four primary standing times, sunrise, sunset, noon and midnight, and what organ Chi is active during each cycle.

Sunrise - Large Intestine
This is the Yangming time we spoke of earlier.

Noon - Heart
The abundance of Yang, therefore the Heart Yang, the spirit of vitality.

Sunset - Kidneys
There's a reason the color associated with the Kidneys is dark blue or

black. This is the onset of night and the increasing abundance of Yin energy. The Kidneys are home to our Essence as well as our root Yin and Yang.

Midnight - Gall Bladder
This time is the apex of the Yin energy. This is interesting because the Gall Bladder is a Yang organ. But one of its lesser known functions is also to act as a catalyst that helps balance all the other chemical reactions in the body. This idea of acting as a catalyst is a Yin function and an example of the fact that there are Yin and Yang elements within each organ.

In addition, the Gall Bladder's paired Yin organ, the Liver is intimately linked with this process. According to Chinese philosophy, the *Hun* or Ethereal soul is housed in the Liver. This is the part of us that is said to survive after death and return to heaven, *Tian*. It rests there during the day and becomes active at night or when we sleep. This pairing of Yin and Yang Organs is known as *Zang Fu.*

The five Zang organs, the Heart (including the Pericardium), Lung, Spleen, Liver, and Kidneys, primarily manufacture and store Essence, that is, Chi, blood, and body fluid. The six Fu organs, the Gall Bladder, Stomach, Large Intestine, Small Intestine, Urinary Bladder and the *Sanjiao* (Triple Burner) basically receive and digest food, absorb nutrient substances, transmit and excrete wastes. The ancient text, the *Suwen* (Basic Questions) states that the five Zang organs store up essential Chi and regulate its outflow while the six Fu organs transform and transport substances without storing them. This interconnected pairing is an important concept to be aware of as we begin to regulate and balance the Yin and Yang during our Zhan Zhuang training.

## NOTE ON THE TEMPERATURES OF CHI

During the days or weeks when we first start practicing, at some point we begin to feel the signs of the Chi. These are signs mind you, not the Chi itself. The most common feeling is a sensation of warmth. And as we progress, this sensation can grow to become quite hot. Some think that's all there is to it, but as one continues from intermediate to advanced levels, over the years, the energies in the body have a chance to balance themselves out.

At that point, the Chi, rather than being hot or cold becomes what we might describe as lukewarm or body temperature. So eventually you don't feel that the Chi raises the temperature of your body because your body has become acclimatized to this heightened state.

A master practitioner can manipulate various qualities of the Chi making it extremely hot or cold, like wind, like water or to create numbness, hardness, softness and stop blood flow. These sort of practices require years of *Nei Kung* training and rely heavily on the calmness of the mind and the focus of the *Yi*, and *Shen*, which must control the whole process.

Now, there are normal hot and cold or warm and cool sensations which come and go when one is first initiated into Zhan Zhuang. Most of these tend to be superficial, more in the muscles or toward the surface of the body. Cool temperatures tend to indicate a circulation deficiency. Warmer temperatures point to excess conditions, like Heat or stagnation. We're speaking of real *heat* here, not just the pleasant warmth, stemming from unimpeded Chi flow.

There are also other qualities that may manifest from time to time during healing and opening up. One of these is wind, which comes about as a result of fire, often due to internal organ imbalance. Fire creates wind and the wind rises, so this type of wind shows up in the head and upper body. But wind can also be felt in the limbs. This type of wind is a result of the increased Chi flow scouring out blockages and is often accompanied by alternating tingling or numbness.

In addition to heat, cold and wind, there is also the sensation of water or liquid, often times moving. The first time I felt this, I had just finished a Zhan Zhuang session and was sitting with a cup of coffee, watching TV. All of a sudden, there was a feeling of warm water running down my leg. Of course, my first thought was, 'Oh, I spilled my coffee.' But when I looked down, my pant leg was dry and my cup of coffee undisturbed. Strange, but true. The feeling was that concrete.

So, there are times when particular areas in the body may react, independent of the whole. For example, during the Zhan Zhuang healing process, an afflicted joint may get very warm during practice. This is often due to an increase in local circulation, which facilitates better blood flow. In addition to that, the warmth can also create a sense of relaxation, like a jacuzzi easing tight muscles and loosening up tendons and ligaments.

This might be considered a physical manifestation of the internal process of 'How Zhan Zhuang Expands Awareness' where a peripheral problem comes to conscious perception under the magnifying glass of standing meditation.

Ultimately, if one stands for a long time and perhaps also practices Taoist alchemy, it is possible to transform what was at the beginning, warmth or heat, into pure light. This is possible because heat and light are born of the same Essence. Within heat is the potential for light and within light there is the potential for heat.

## HOW ZHAN ZHUANG EXPANDS AWARENESS

For the sake of this discussion, think of body awareness as three interconnected segments. (see diagram) Imagine three concentric circles, each linked to one another. Now put yourself in the center of the innermost circle. This circle represents our conscious awareness, what we can actually feel. The second circle represents our peripheral feeling awareness, what we can just barely feel, sense or glimpse. And the third circle represents what is at present out of range, what we cannot yet feel or perceive.

What happens over time in Zhan Zhuang practice, is that parts of the second circle (our peripheral feeling-awareness) become magnified to the point that they fuse with our conscious awareness. (the first circle) At the same time, elements of the third circle are amplified enough to move into the second circle. (our peripheral awareness)

This cycle continues to play out again and again and with each round our conscious awareness grows, sometimes exponentially. In addition, our body becomes stronger and more healthy.

The amazing thing about Zhan Zhuang is that everyone who practices daily will inevitably gain such expansions and all the benefits that go with them, including profound improvement in their Tai Chi form and Push Hands.

Such being the case, don't be surprised if on the way to heal one thing, you find new things surface that you didn't even know were there. *The first step in correcting an imbalance is knowing of it's existence.*

This is how our kinesthetic sense of perception works. 'You don't know you've been in jail until they let you out.' That means, you didn't realize there was a problem or blockage until it let go or was resolved. Also, it's important to note that when such a blockage, often long-standing, decides to let go it's much like when a child makes a fist and squeezes it for as long as they can. When they finally let go, their fingers and hand suddenly feel weak.

So, after such 'letting-go' experiences, it often happens the affected area feels weak, vulnerable or without the same strength as the adjoining regions. After all, it's been holding tension, similar to the child's fist, for who knows how long.

Now, all that is part of the physical side of the body's transformation. But what about the more subtle aspects of perception that have and will come into play? How will they effect our body awareness as well as the emotions, mind and spirit?

As a result of extensive Zhan Zhuang practice, the mind learns to be patient and calm, and as it becomes more quiescent, various emotions and cellular memories flood to the surface for reexamination and resolution. Usually these past experiences or injuries will re-manifest almost exactly as they were. This can often freak out the novice practitioner but the good news is, the manifestation is only *temporary*. After a few minutes, hours or in some more severe cases, days, the imbalance will suddenly disappear or gradually fade into emptiness.

Usually this has to do with a letting go in some manner, for it is only after our conscious and subconscious baggage has been resolved, that we can count on our increased perception to be clear and accurate.

All this most certainly has an effect on one's spirit or true self and the liberation thereof. This means the freedom to explore our connection, both with the things of this world, and also what lies beyond.

# HOW ZHAN ZHUANG EXPANDS AWARENESS

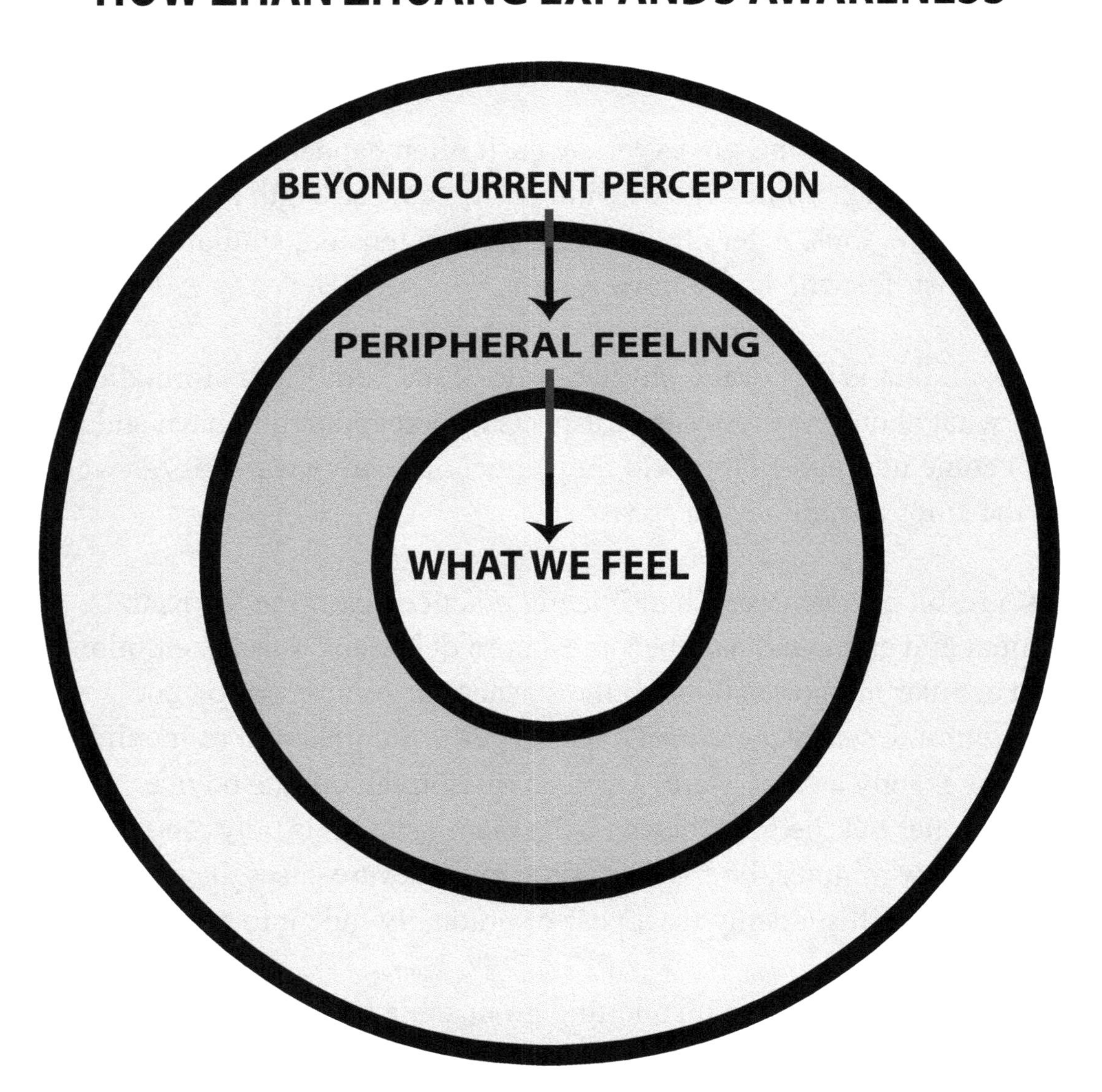


**The Three Circles of Awareness**

## INVESTIGATING THE NATURE OF RELAXATION

In essence, what we are doing in Zhan Zhuang practice is investigating the nature of relaxation. However, relaxation in this case is not simply becoming limp, for if we completely relax all our muscles, we will certainly fall down. Therefore, the type of relaxation we're looking for involves the minimum dynamic tension required to hold the body upright.

After much practice, our equilibrium becomes very refined and we are able to 'balance on the bones.' At that point, the perceived dynamic tension of the body's soft tissue, becomes virtually nil. This deep relaxation will eventually permeate even further and include the organs, glands and even the brain.

Why is this important? Because so much of one's progress literally comes from deeper and deeper relaxation. *Wang Xiang Zhai*, the creator of *Yiquan*, was clear about the necessity for personal investigation and experimentation in this regard. So what are the components of relaxation and how can we deepen them?

Relaxation has three basic components: physical, energetic and mental. The physical involves the loosening and letting go of muscular and/or structural tension within the body. The second physical factor is the breath which after first becoming slow and even at the earlier stages, then becomes long and slender and sometimes seems to disappear altogether. This regulating the breath has the effect of calming the nerves as well as slowing the mind and ameliorating the emotions.

We will now address the mind itself, for without its proper regulation, deep relaxation is simply not possible. The mind is meant to be a servant, but with so many people it ends up being the master. This often leads to unwanted consequences. So for genuine relaxation to occur, the mind must be brought to heel.

The mind can be devious however, so some trickery in the way of substitution will be in order. If we command the mind to be quiet, chances are we'll get just the opposite, increased thought patterns and mental tension. So, what to do?

The answer lies first with breath regulation which, when done correctly, will slow the entire thought process. But even that isn't enough. The way is to remove our attention from the mind and thought altogether. The easiest way to do this is to substitute pure feeling. Only concentrate on *feeling* what's going on, and not thinking about it or judging it.

There is another way, an advanced method which involves withdrawing our consciousness into the secret spot or center of the brain. By holding our awareness there, the mind and thought take on a peripheral aspect which can be discarded through single-pointed focus.

So we have a calm body and a long, slender breath, balanced or neutral emotions and a placid mind free from chaos, but there's still other factors when it comes to relaxation.

Those factors could be termed acceptance and comfort. Accepting one's self for just who one is, in other words, being comfortable with who you are in the present moment. And that includes all aspects of one's personality and being.

As regards comfort, in the final analysis, it is the feeling of increasing comfort that acts as a gauge to measure the deeper and deeper states of relaxation.

## TRANSFORMATION OF NERVES AND SINEWS

One of the most amazing things that happens in Zhan Zhuang is the change that can take place in the nerves and also, in the tissues where the nerves are located. What is this change?

A physical transformation within the nerve sheaths. And as a result, something happens through extensive training that makes the nerves both more sensitive, and at the same time, less subconsciously reactive to outer stimuli.

For the masses, a sudden, unexpected stimulus inevitably creates a 'knee-jerk' reaction, an involuntary movement often accompanied by unwanted tension. It is easy to see that in a self-defense situation, this subconscious reactive response could spell disaster. Instead, when confronted, something very different happens to the adept.

The serious practitioner becomes calmer, more centered and ready to react instantly. The degree of relaxation is often in direct proportion to the strength of the threat. The greater the threat or tension, the greater the relaxed centeredness.

It is said that the *Yang Chi* is finite, whereas the *Yin Chi* is infinite. That means our ability to generate *Yin Chi*, the relaxed, centered readiness state, can always be greater than the finite *Yang Chi* threat. Here we can glimpse the origin of the Classics regarding the knowledge that most encounters are decided before combat is ever joined. We're talking about winning the battle first, inside ourselves.

The transformation of the nerves also affects the sinews, that is, the muscles, tendons, ligaments and fascia. The reestablishing of original nerve firing sequences creates repetitive connective elongation and condensation, which energizes the entire muscle, rather than primarily the muscle belly as traditional strength training and weight-lifting tend to do.

This elongation has a direct effect on the speed of the transmission of nerve messages (impulses) making the connection and response of the brain much like a highly trained professional athlete. Out here in Hawaii people like to paddle. (ocean padding in large canoes) It's interesting to note that often the strongest paddler in the boat, the one with the greatest consistency and endurance is the wiry one, not the bulked up one. Now you can see why.

Another aspect in this transformation is the smoothness factor, the seamless integration and cooperative functioning of the body's tissues made possible by hardwiring and lengthy repetitive practice. This leads to elements of unified movement discussed earlier.

Of course the muscles cannot actually fuse or unify physically but energetically, it is another matter. When this element of energetic unification occurs, it feels like whole sections of the body or the entire body itself, is working as one big piece, in other words, Spherical Movement or some aspect thereof.

There is still another arena regarding the transformation of the nerves and sinews which needs to be discussed. And that is the healing aspect and Zhan Zhuang's uncanny ability to, over time, rejuvenate and restart the proper functioning of injured nerves along with damaged tissues.

This happens to a large extent, due to the greatly enhanced bio-electromagnetic energy or Chi, flowing and surging throughout the region during one's practice. You might liken it to giving your car battery a jump-start, only increasing to the optimum voltage very gradually over a long period of time.

Sometimes these moments feel like little jolts as the brain tests to see if a region is capable of sustaining a stronger amount of electrical current necessary for the smooth elocution of movement. This is when some part of the body jerks involuntarily. These involuntary twitches, can also signal the body's attempt to open up muscle blockages due to tension or injury.

That brings us to the matter of the tendons and ligaments, which western medicine claims are largely un-fixable once damaged. Under ordinary circumstances this may be true, but with the Zhan Zhuang practitioner, these sinews undergo a unique form of transformation, healing and recovery. Tendons out of balance tend to be shortened, lengthened or 'frozen,' that is, very hard and inflexible.

Shortening or lengthening can occur as a result of some mechanical injury or, shortening can be due to inadequate nourishment of blood, oxygen or nutrients. This usually stems from a Liver Chi imbalance. This 'starvation' can also contribute to frozen, largely immobile tendons or ligaments and therefore, stiffness in the joints.

Much of the tendons healing process occurs through rapid nerve firing that creates a shaking, or bouncing mechanism in the case of ligaments, that is, feeling the whole body or large portions of it, cycle with almost wild motion. This can have the effect of loosening, stretching and lengthening what is too tight, as well as tightening and condensing what has been over-stretched and lacks the proper tensile strength. The good news is, prolonged Zhan Zhuang practice can slowly bring back much of the elasticity necessary to move normally. I can personally attest to this.

## OPENING AND CLOSING

Traditionally, the opening and closing of the joints, sometimes called pulsing the joints, was taught as a second stage in Tai Chi training, following the mastering of postural alignments.

The method finds its origin in the Universal Pulse or Breath, that is, the natural cyclical expansion and condensation of all things in the physical universe.

Once opening and closing of the joints and cavities (thoracic and abdominal) is mastered, this natural pulse generally becomes active during all our meditation and relaxed practices.

So, what is opening and closing? In terms of the joints, it is the expanding and condensing of all the tissues surrounding the joint, but the actual initiatory factor stems from a centerpoint deep inside. This has to do, not only with expanding and condensing, but also the increasing or decreasing of the pressure in the joints. (synovial fluid)

This central juncture is found in the dead center of each joint and is derived from the intersection of two lines; one from front to back and the other from inside to the outside of the joint. The point where the two lines intersect is what you're looking and feeling for.

There is a misconception about opening and closing the joints that concerns the size of the movements. The fact is the movements of the individual joints are small and must be restricted to very small as the skill is being learned. Otherwise there is danger of damaging the joint through excessive stretching of tendons and particularly the ligaments. What makes the overall movement of opening and closing the joints and cavities appear bigger than it really is, is the combined linkage.

In other words, all parts working simultaneously in harmony, moving together.

The easiest way to properly begin working up the method is to isolate each particular joint. It is easiest to begin with the upper joints, specifically the elbow, wrist and hand. The following exercise is a safe way to begin getting a handle on what opening and closing is, and what it should actually feel like.

Sit down at your kitchen table or the like and position yourself so the bottom of your elbow, the forearm and the side of the hand are solidly on the table.

Now, place your opposite hand on the elbow crease such that you can feel some of the tendons and muscle attachments, while still being able to pin the elbow firmly to the table, so the bone doesn't move.

Next, transfer your feeling-awareness from the elbow, down through the forearm and wrist, and as you do, stretch the forearm muscles toward the wrist, stretch the wrist into the hand, stretch the hand into the fingers and also stretch the hand slightly laterally. And finally, extend and elongate each of the joints of the fingers and thumb.

All this must be done in such a way, that is with small movements, so the elbow bone, which you've been holding down, doesn't move forward.

If the bone *does* slide forward, it means some or all of the individual movements were too big or, you weren't applying sufficient downward pressure with the opposite hand. Notice we do each of the motions one after another, from the elbow to the finger tips.

Later, this will be simultaneous, with each joint moving at their own independent frequency, but beginning and ending together.

Now it's time to reverse the procedure and condense or retract the joints of the fingers back into the hand, and the palm back into the wrist. The combination of these two condensing movements create what's known as a "tile hand," based on the shape of a Chinese roofing tile. From there, we stretch the wrist back into the forearm and the forearm muscles back into the elbow joint. (from the extremities into the center)

This is the most basic exercise. Later you will include the shoulder and shoulder blade, the spine, torso and lower extremities. This same upper extremity technique can also be adapted to the lower body using the hips, knees and ankles, then later adding the Kua. After all this has been mastered, twisting, wrapping and spiraling the tissues is then added to generate Spiral Opening and Closing. Of course, the inevitable goal is to link the whole body, including all its tissues, organs and bones, to the Universal pulse at a cellular level. At that level, the cells can perform three types of movement activity. They can expand or open, they can condense or close, or they can freeze, becoming rigid and seemingly immobile. This relates to the actual issuing of power in certain types of Fa Jing.

The basic upper body linkage is as follows. The spine out through the shoulder blade, shoulder, upper arm, elbow, forearm, wrist, hand and fingers. The lower body linkage includes the Kua, hips, thighs, knees, lower leg, ankles and feet. Once you have hardwired each separately, its time to use the Six External Harmonies to connect them.

Of course, later this must include the spine, torso, neck and head as well. In other words, 'whole body opening and closing.' At that point the diligent Tai Chi practitioner will apply this to every movement and transition in their form in order to achieve the second level of competence, The first being the mastering of alignments.

There are many variations of opening and closing. For instance, we can work with the descending energy, releasing downward. When using this method, any tension or dis-ease, will fall to the Station below the region we're releasing. We can also work with the ascending energy, releasing upward. With this method, any tension or dis-ease tends to temporarily gather in the Station *above* where we're working. Once these downward and upward techniques have been mastered separately, it's time to combine them. This skill is an absolute necessity for higher level Tai Chi and Fa Jing. These advanced methods are essentially predicated on going from our center to our extremities, (expanding, opening) and then returning from our extremities back into our center. (condensing, closing)

**Vertical Method**

The combined vertical method involves opening and closing in two directions simultaneously. Opening from our centerpoint up to our head (and hands) and from our centerpoint down to our feet. Closing reverses the process, from above and below back into our center.

**Horizontal Method**

The combined horizontal method involves bilateral opening and closing. From our centerline out to the sides of our body, and then return. When you merge both methods, you get what you would expect, Spherical Opening and Closing, that is, opening from our centerpoint and expanding in all directions simultaneously until we reach the ends of our energy-body, which is itself a larger sphere. This is of course, followed by retraction back into our center. It is the repetition of this cycle that initiates Spherical Whole Body Pulsing.

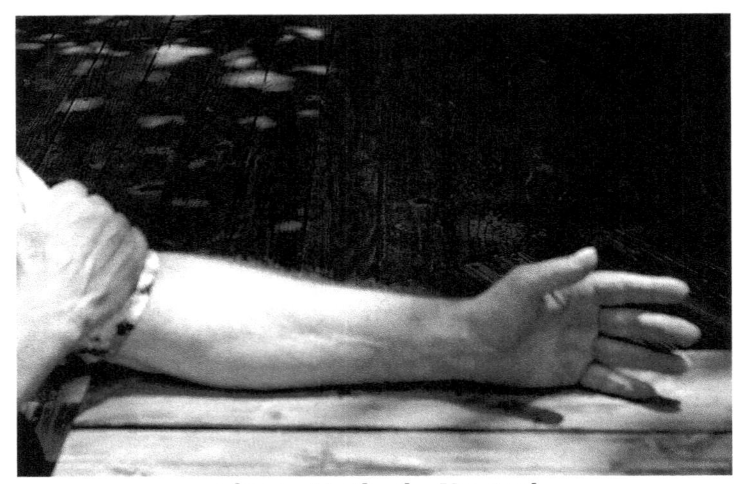

**Linear Method - Neutral**

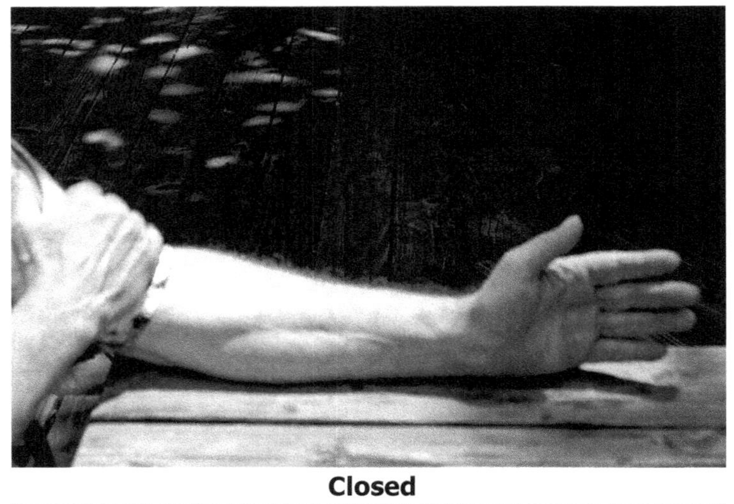

**Closed**

**Open**

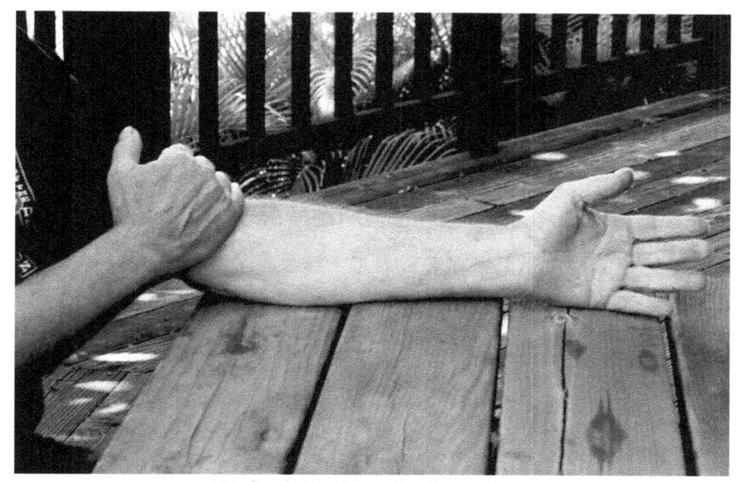

**Spiral Method - Neutral**

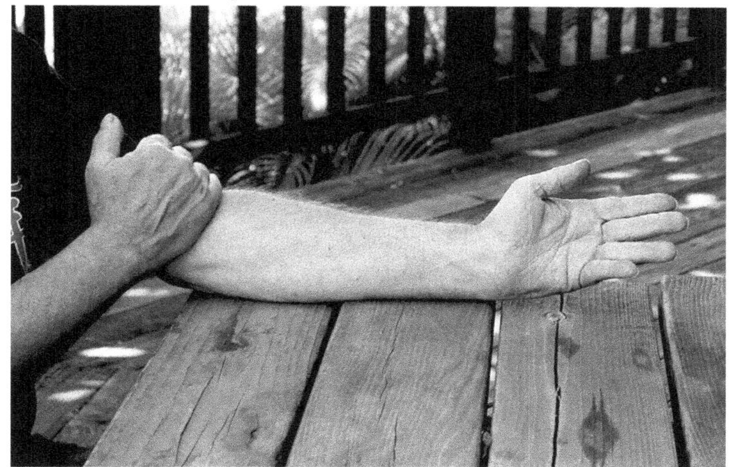

**Closed**

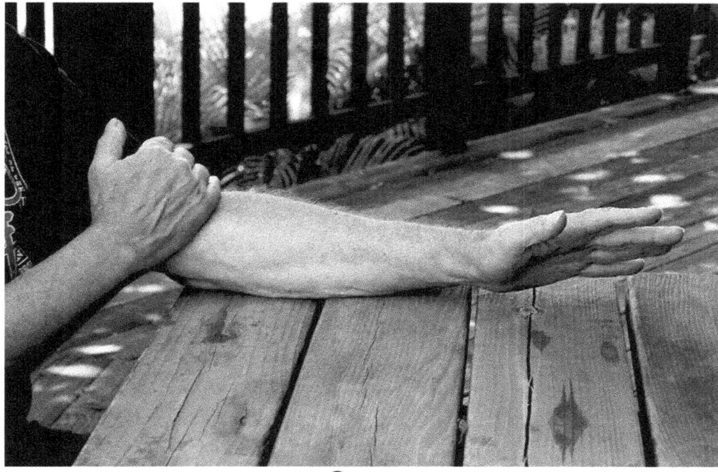

**Open**

## WORKING WITH SPIRAL ENERGY

Spiral energy is one of nature's most intrinsic forms of movement. It consists of a combination of Yin and Yang, or circling force, joined with straight-line force. The outward projecting, straight-line force (*Ji)* is considered Yang, while the circular, rotating force is considered Yin.

It is the combination of these two energies that not only creates awesome power, but also scours the body and its pathways imbuing them with abundant healing power.

There are basically two types of spirals, *Wei*, outgoing, or *Nei,* incoming. Both types utilize straight line movement combined with circular movement. Chen style Tai Chi delves deeply into this practice. Here we're speaking of external spirals, motions you can see.

But there is another type of spiral that is perhaps even more important and that is the *Nei Kung* or internal spiraling energy.

In terms of Tai Chi, there should be some spiral energy in every movement. Chen style spirals are the most overt. In the Yang style, spirals are present, but not always so obvious and in the Northern Wu style, they are almost completely internal, barely visible, if at all.

When training the upper extremities, we can use the same basic sequence that was used with opening and closing, but now, this will be expanded to include turning or spiraling. Spiraling here implies either an outgoing extension (opening) or an incoming condensing. (closing)

The basic sequence of the outgoing upper extremities rotation is as follows. The Central Channel and Spine, out to the chest and back including the Pectoralis Major and Minor, the Shoulder Blade and

Teres muscles, the shoulder, upper arm, elbow, forearm, wrist, hand and fingers. The incoming method works in reverse, beginning with the fingers and ending up in the Spine and Central Channel.

For lower body outgoing spiraling, we start in the low Dan Tien, Kua, Sacrum and buttocks, then to the hips and thighs, the knees and muscles of the lower leg, the ankles and the feet. Again reverse the procedure to generate the incoming spirals.

When first exploring all this, its best to start with simple turning, if only to loosen things up. Let's use the incoming upper extremity method as our example.

Start with the arm extended. Rotate your fingers, hand and wrist in an incoming direction, retracting or telescoping the elbow, shoulder and shoulder blade back into the spine. (from the extremities into your center) This rotation can be either clockwise or counterclockwise.

Now, whereas the fingers, hand and wrist moved on relatively the same plane, elements of the elbow, shoulder, and shoulder blade will want to rotate on different planes.

It is the integration of each of these variegated frequencies that generates the power buildup or Chi amplification necessary for dynamic *Jing*. In the case of *Nei Chan Ssu Jin*, (inward silk reeling) this would be in terms of neutralization of an attack, and would be felt by the opponent as being pulled in and stuck to whatever part of your body intercepted the blow.

Now in order for this to happen, all parts of one's spiraling must be fully hardwired to the low Dan Tien. This also implies Dan Tien Rotation.

So, in the whole-body outgoing method, spiraling begins in the Dan Tien, then moves out until it reaches the bottoms of the feet and the tips of the fingers.

With this type of spiraling, the body is often divided into left and right halves. While the defending side executes incoming spirals, the attacking side simultaneously performs outgoing spirals. This basic division of Yin and Yang *is* Tai Chi.

When these methods are practiced, they are executed smoothly and gracefully, coming all the way in and going all the way out in concert. This generates a loose single or double whole body spiral. After much repetition this will look like the slithering of a snake.

Once the movements are fluid, it's time to add the *Nei Kung* element. *Nei Kung* spiraling can greatly amplify the full power, whiplike release of our Fa Jing. Whereas the body can only turn and spiral in so many different directions, and the linkage required dictates the end result is a rather big movement considering, Nei Kung spiraling has no such limitations.

After first hardwiring through meditation the ability to feel and generate spiral energy around every limb as well as the torso, head and neck, we can then learn to regulate both the speed and the number of revolutions, thereby creating a 'dimmer-switch' of sorts which we can then use to control the amount of outgoing or incoming energy.

With enough practice it becomes possible to generate rapid, powerful *Nei Kung* spirals and discharge them with only a small gesture such as a flick of the wrist.

## WORKING WITH SPHERICAL ENERGY

Spherical energy, which is really the development of the spherical energy body is one of the great benefits of Zhan Zhuang practice. It begins to naturally occur when enough of the body's external and internal tissues have become energetically unified.

The importance of sphericality stems from several factors. The first is its roundness and evenness. From the health point of view, this speaks to the smooth and even distribution of the Chi flow, throughout the organism. It is said where the Chi is flowing and abundant, dis-ease cannot light.

From an internal martial arts viewpoint, think of the body like a ball filled with water. If pressure (an attack) is exerted on one side of the ball, there is a reaction on the opposite side of the ball. This reaction absorbs and neutralizes the pressure which is then 'rebounded' back to its source along one of nearly an infinite number of arcs or circuitous vectors.

Think about it. A sphere is essentially composed of a near infinite number of circles, intersecting on different planes. This means that an incoming blow can be diverted or absorbed without compromising one's centerline and then rerouted back to the opponent via a totally unexpected angle.

Besides the health and martial arts aspects, spherical energy is also a product of more and more of our total consciousness becoming focused to a single concentrated point. This sphericality is the body's natural and most efficient operational state. Therefore, it represents the body following the line of least resistance.

Many years ago when I was first starting out, I lucked into an experience which when I described it to my older training brothers, made them very jealous. They told me, “People can go through many years of training and never experience that.” It was only years later, that I realized what had truly happened.

I was about three months into my daily practice, when one day, while doing my usual morning stand, something amazing happened.

I was focusing on my centerpoint behind the navel area and successfully narrowed my focus such that I began to feel an intense heat growing from that tiny single point.

Suddenly the heat vanished and I could see and feel within myself. I watched as the single point of light located in my center, rapidly grew into a cylinder throughout my torso.

Then, almost as quickly as it appeared, the cylinder expanded in all directions until it formed a sphere inside and outside of my body. I don’t know how long I watched (from inside the center of the sphere) and felt it, but when the experience was over, a part of me knew where my transformation would lead.

At this point I must stress that this was only a ‘glimpse,’ meaning it would be years ’till I could consciously enter into a similar experience.

The concept of ‘glimpses’ is worth talking about, because it will occur for many practitioners during different stages of development.

The idea is that during our stand, our body-mind consciousness almost stumbles into a higher level of awareness and for a short time we are able to know, see and feel, a more relaxed and efficient state of being.

Unfortunately, we are generally unable to maintain or recreate this state of consciousness. After all, that's why it's called a glimpse. That said, a part of the experience will definitely remain with us and can be used as a good starting point for deeper achievement.

Think of these glimpses as signposts of things to come. They can occur almost anytime and anywhere. We don't necessarily have to be practicing Zhan Zhuang or Tai Chi to open up and receive these sort of insights and experiences.

At this point, at the risk of being obvious, I must point out that the physical body itself can never actually become spherical. If it could, we would all look something like amoebas.

The roundness, curves, arcs and circles we use in the Zhan Zhuang postures and Tai Chi movements, are *intimations and tracings of parts of the energetic sphere*. In other words, the sphericality of the developed energy body. This is one of the reasons the Classics advise us to keep the mind (and the majority of our feeling-awareness) in the Dan Tien during Tai Chi practice.

Though our bodies can only fold, bend and twist to certain degrees and in certain directions, while going through the Tai Chi form we can use our mind and feeling-awareness to spherically expand and condense our subtle bodies energetically, as we move through the postures.

If we believe the Taoist sages of antiquity, who supposedly had the ability to see inside the human body, life forms from a single point of light which expands to become the Kidneys, brain and spinal cord, followed by the rest of the body. And that single point is actually a miniature DNA-filled sphere.

## USING THE PHYSICAL TO INFLUENCE THE MIND

Just as we can use mental relaxation to calm the body, we can also use elements of physical relaxation to calm the mind.

We've already spoken briefly about regulating the breath, that is making the inhale and the exhale each last the same amount of time. When starting out, it's best to follow the body's natural rhythm to determine how many seconds the inhale and exhale should be. Five seconds in and five seconds out or ten seconds in and ten seconds out and so forth.

The first key to this is picking a length of time that does not use up all your air, either on the inhale or the exhale. If you run out of breath, the Perineal region will contract and you will have created tension rather than relaxation.

The second key is to be flexible and be willing to adapt as the body changes. For example, if we start with five seconds in and five seconds out, after a few cycles we might find that the body has the capacity to breathe a little longer so, the natural thing to do is extend the length of each phase, say to seven or eight seconds each.

Conversely, one might be utilizing ten seconds in and ten seconds out when suddenly, for no apparent reason, this length feels too long. The thing to do then, is simply follow the body's lead and reduce the length of each cycle to eight or even seven seconds per phase.

Actually, this type of reaction does have a reason, and may occur when the body is dealing with a blockage and needs more Chi energy to do so. Many times this can simply be the result of the work you're doing.

Regulating the breath in the above manner, that is, making it even, will in turn soothe and slow the mind. In other words, it will generally reduce the intensity of one's thoughts and many times even out or balance one's feelings as well.

While the above technique is essentially a *Chi Kung* method, the second technique is purely *Nei Kung*. The second method works exactly opposite to the previous one, that is, we make no effort to regulate the breath at all, but simply observe it. We may find that the body changes the length of each cycle, or some cycles seem to be even for a while and then things change.

Whatever it is, we just observe and make no attempt to influence or alter what is happening. What we are in fact doing with this type of method where the breath is ignored, is utilizing our single-pointed focus on either a specific action, location or feeling. In this case, the feeling of being relaxed while being aware of our breath.

Another technique along these lines is to pick a place in the body that clearly feels relaxed and loose. Simply focus on feeling this region, to the exclusion of all else. After a few moments, the physical relaxation will start to 'rub off' on the mind, who's activity will then begin to recede.

In addition to the breath, there are also specific physical locations that can help relax the mind. The first is the eyes, where we work on relaxing all the eye muscles and then settle our feeling-awareness toward the back of the eyeball, where the optic nerve connects. Relaxing this area slows the rate of both nerve messages and thoughts.

Another location that can influence the mind is the temples. The actual point we can activate is called *Taiyang* point, in the center of the soft tissue of the temple. This region can have a direct and powerful effect on the mind. It can sometimes 'open' the mind, that is, connect it to the energies of the external environment, in which case thought simply seems to cease, at least temporarily.

There is another technique that I used at a certain point in my Zhan Zhuang training that was very effective. Upon awakening, while I was still drowsy and my mind had not yet kicked into high gear, I would stumble out to my mat and begin my morning stand.

That's really all there is to it. What makes this so effective, is that by carrying over the body relaxation of the sleep state into our Zhan Zhuang meditation, there is far less mental and emotional baggage running around inside our heads and therefore less interference with our feeling-awareness, focus and concentration.

## THE POSITION OF THE EYES

The use of the eyes in Zhan Zhuang, depends upon one's goals. There are three basic positions, open, closed and half-open, half-closed. The closed position is used for health and healing, and also for deeper forms of meditation. The open position is used for martial arts and certain advanced energy healing techniques. The half-open, half-closed methods are used for different types of meditation.

Let's discuss the eyes open methods. First of all, what you *don't* want to do is to stare blankly and mindlessly into space. So, for martial arts, we have several options, all of which require at least some use of the peripheral vision. The simplest method is to choose a point on the ground about six to ten feet in front of you.

With the majority of your visual attention focused there, use your peripheral vision to become aware of the wide field surrounding your focal point. Having a fully developed peripheral vision is an important asset in combat.

In the second method, we will change the focus to some distant object or point. Now, while holding your attention there, engage your peripheral vision or what some have termed, 'Eagle Vision.' One activates their peripheral vision by somewhat relaxing the eye muscles while at the same time relaxing and broadening their field of focus.

When you get good at this you can even 'see' beyond 180 degrees, in other words, partly behind you. A variation of this is to gaze into the distance with your eyes looking straight ahead at the horizon, but with no specific focal point. This means to diffuse your focus away from any single point or thing. This kind of seeing can put you more in touch with the energies of your subtle bodies and develops both inward and outward concentration. Another reason for this sort of cultivation is that at very high levels, the eyes are indispensable in the projection of energy and power.

A simple example of this, is the third method, which is projecting and drawing in Chi, using the horizon. For this, we will also coordinate the breath to help, until our *Nei Kung* ability alone is sufficient.

Relax and focus out to the horizon line. Now inhale, and as you do, slowly withdraw your visual attention closer and closer to your body. Then, using your 'inner seeing,' draw the visual energy you just brought with you (from the horizon) into your body and specifically into your Central Channel and from there down into the low Dan Tien.

Now, let's turn our attention to the eyes-closed methods. For health, the idea of closing the eyes is that it returns or recycles our energy inward, back into the system.

Closed eyes also make focusing inside easier (less distractions) and in my experience is useful no matter what your goal. With all methods, it is important to retain great relaxation in the eye muscles.

And this is especially true for the back of the eyeball, where it joins the optic nerve. Learning to relax this location alone, can have a profound calming effect on the entire body, nervous system and mind.

With the eyes-closed methods, there are generally three focal points for our inner vision from which to choose. They are the low Dan Tien, the upper Dan Tien and what I'll call a soft or diffused focus, which means not really using the eyes in a normal manner at all. The first two are fairly obvious.

Since our physical and in a sense, our inner vision, are in the head area, to get to the low Dan Tien, we relax the eyeballs downward as though going to sleep and then simply 'look down' into the area where the Dan Tien would be in the physical body. Unlike our physical eyes, with our inner vision, there will be no tissue to obstruct our view.

For the upper Dan Tien, the method is even easier, since we're already right there. Simply gaze straight ahead, close your eyes and relax them like going to sleep, while maintaining your inner vision steady on the horizon of your 'inner screen.'

One wants to cultivate what can be termed a soft or oblique focus. In other words not too tightly narrowed.

The next method is exactly the opposite. Close your eyes and focus on a single point somewhere near the center of your inner vision and just hold it there.

This kind of seeing - using one's inner visual attention rather than what the physical eyes see - has its basis in the Taoist axiom of *Wu Wei* and is used in such practices as 'Circulation of the Light.

And finally, there is the diffuse method in which you close your eyes and don't try to see anything. Instead you ignore the visuals, whatever they are, and switch to pure feeling and hold onto that. This technique can often generate a powerful new body awareness.

Now to the Half-Inside/Half-Outside Method. This has to do with the position of the eyelids, which are half-lowered. The key to this type of technique is to be peripherally aware of the objective world, while at the same time focusing the majority of your visual attention within.

First, look straight ahead, into the distance, perhaps out to the horizon, while half-closing your eyes. Let the eyelids relax and get heavy, such that they obscure half your field of vision.

Then, and here's the trick, while keeping your attention focused straight ahead, relax the eye muscles downward like going to sleep.

At this point, your attention, which is still looking straight ahead, will have become focused on your 'inner screen' - eyelids obscuring the upper half of the objective world, while your physical eyes are lightly focused downward on the physical reality.

With this method there are two arenas of focus we can use. The first is the physical reality in the lower half of our vision, the eye-open part. Here we can focus downward, three to six feet or even up to ten feet away. The majority of our visual attention is focused in the physical world, while we are only aware of the upper, eyes-shut half, peripherally.

The other thing we can do, is reverse the process, which is the preferred method for certain types of meditation. In other words, our main area of concentration is the upper, eyes-closed, inner world and we are only aware of the outer world peripherally.

Whichever methods you use, realize that the eyes are a powerful tool and also a powerful distraction. This is equally true for the ears and hearing or listening. That is why in certain advanced practices, one learns how to close these off. We need this 'sealing' in order to enter into the deepest forms of concentration.

## OPENING THE CENTRAL CHANNEL

A major opening of the Central Channel is generally a stupendous event. Although there are a number of long and tedious alchemical methods that aim at inducing it, it's my experience that this achievement has other factors which cannot necessarily be controlled or pidgin-holed. Among these, are the state of one's health, the strength of the internal organs, as well as the individual's emotional balance and current state of consciousness or awareness.

Unlike some other experiences in Zhan Zhuang training, there is no mistaking what happens with this one. The exact manner of the opening can occur in several ways, but there is a common factor. Each involves a strong, undeniable wave or movement of energy, (*Jing*, *Chi*, *Shen*) through the Central Channel. Most of the time this wave begins at the bottom and goes up. However, occasionally the direction of the flow is reversed.

Energy moving up from the bottom of the torso, through *Huiyin* CV-1, and the Earth Point, the spot equidistant between the feet, is considered *Yin*, while the downward flow, from *Baihui* point GV-20 or above, is the descending *Yang* or Heaven energy.

An element of the descending Heaven energy should be very familiar as we work with it from the beginning of our study, when we learn to release blockages downward.

By starting the training with learning how to 'ground' the Heaven energy, or what in it's initial stage is simply balancing the effects of gravity, we are unknowingly preparing the way so that one day when the *Yin* or Earth energy spontaneously rises, we will remain balanced mentally and emotionally and not become like the victims of Kundalini

Yoga for example. In other words you won't go nuts. By that I mean not just mentally unbalanced, schizophrenic and the like, but sometime there is something far more insidious and this has to do with a greatly overinflated sense of power or self importance. Herein lies the wisdom of the Zhan Zhuang method; it literally protects us in the higher practices.

Perhaps my own experience will shed some light on what might be expected, although the details will certainly vary according to the individual.

It happened many years ago. I got up from a good night's sleep and went out for my morning stand. As was my custom at the time, I put on some quiet music which I used to keep track of time rather than wearing a watch.

The music began to play and I settled in, resting my attention in the low Dan Tien. Then sometime later, I'm not exactly sure how long, as the music reached a particularly poignant passage, the energy that had been building in my low Dan Tien suddenly descended out the *Huiyin* point and into the ground below. An instant later it returned, bringing with it the *Yin Chi* of Earth.

Entering *Huiyin* point, the *Yin*, Earth energy began to rise, quickly boring a hollow energetic cylinder all the way up through the top of my head. Simultaneously another energy, almost like volcanic magma began to fill the cylinder from the bottom, only more slowly.

As this energy surged upward, flooding my Dan Tien and lower abdomen, I began to have feelings of invincible martial and sexual power.

As the energy reached my Solar Plexus and the Ancestral Chi point, *Shanzhong* CV-17, its quality transformed into something lighter and more refined. As this energy inundated my chest, I felt my heart open and become filled with the most indescribable feelings.

While in this state, the energy again began to rise, becoming even more refined but without losing its intensity, as it prepared for its ascent to the higher regions.

Then, before you could say, Bob's-your-uncle, this highly refined energy raced upwards through my throat, into my brain where it burst out the top of my head like a water fountain.

Shooting into the air several feet above me and then descending as if surrendering to gravity, the energy fell upon me and through me, like drops of warm rain.

After that, I couldn't speak for a little while. But over the following days, I slowly realized that everything had changed. I began getting flows of energy during Zhan Zhuang practice representing various types of energetic martial movements and the knowingness of how to use them. These feelings were literally happening inside my body.

To put it another way, many of the concepts mentioned in the Classics which were only 'book learning' to a certain extent up 'till then, started becoming bona fide realities that I could manifest at will. Not only that, the amount of energy infused into the spinal cord reaches *every* aspect of the physical body and sometimes spontaneous healings are possible. But even if not, the amount of life-force engendered, invigorates the body, mind and emotions in such a way that we are never quite the same.

## ENTERING THE VOID

When one achieves a considerable amount of genuine relaxation, it sometimes happens that they experience a 'time warp,' a sort of space/time distortion. *Wang Xiang Zhai* called it entering the Void.

The Void is a Buddhist term, Taoists call it Emptiness. The word void is a little bit of a misnomer in that it means 'without contents or empty.' This can be taken to refer to structure or form as we know form, meaning empty of things we can grasp with the mind.

There is an intrinsic difficulty in describing something that is beyond the ken of the mind. Using words, images and mental constructs can only convey an echo of the real thing. After all, we're speaking of experiences in pure beingness, beyond our natural boundaries of time and space.

But the fact that there is nothing 'recognizable,' doesn't mean that this state is inert. On the contrary, in one sense, these states of higher awareness are constantly in motion, only in *present time*.

This means we don't have the usual linear reference points by which to measure our experience, let alone time or space. But even so, we can still have a knowingness. The first awareness of this sort usually occurs after the fact.

For example, we think we've been standing for 15 or 20 minutes, but when we check the time, it turns out to be closer to 40 or 50 minutes. When this occurs, it feels like our blood sparkles like champagne and we're filled with vitality.

Some of the other signs may be the absence of thought and even emotion, little or no awareness of the physical body combined with the sense of perceiving and being part of the subtle nonphysical energies. Also, there may be a calmness or peacefulness that seems to pervade the depth of our being.

Under certain circumstances, especially if one is using one of the eyes-closed methods, it is possible to have a completely non-corporeal experience. When this happens, sometimes we can recollect much, if not all of the event, while other times the impression rapidly fades.

These and the other types of experiences mentioned will inevitably lead to what we might call 'complete absorption' such that the experiencer and what is being experienced are indistinguishable. Some call this Samadhi.

These experiences by their nature, resonate through one's entire being and therefore can have a strong balancing effect on the mind and emotions, not to mention some feelings of ecstasy. Physically this ecstasy often stems from the fact that the energy that has flooded our being, makes the body feel like its running like a well-oiled machine, smoothly, effortlessly.

After decades of practice, one can sometimes sense when they are about to enter into one of these states, although each experience is at least to some degree unique.

Once again, entering the Void is not an experience that we can plan for or even directly encourage, except for being willing to go beyond our own limitations, that is, what we know and what we *think we know*. These states of awareness are gifts and when you experience one, afterwards, it's important to be grateful.

## WORKING WITH LIGHT

As far as Zhan Zhuang is concerned, this is a subject that generally doesn't come up until after decades of practice, if at all. Have you ever been in a darkened room and then closed your eyes and instead of the total blackness you might expect, there is some form of light or color, sometimes in patterns on your inner screen?

Scientists give all kinds of reasons for this, having to do with the brain and the way the eye functions, but there is more to it than that. Regarding inner light, according to the mystics, there are also color correspondences with the various energy centers located in the Spine and Central Channel.

In ancient times, part of the advanced training was to be sequestered in a cave for varying periods of time. This was done so the candidate would literally have to face all his or her demons and the illusions that go with them. The light manifesting during this part of the overall procedure would often be of the darker, lower vibrational hues.

The idea was after enough time these phantasms would go away and the individual would find themselves face to face with the indestructible, ever-present, light of reality. This light can come in various colors like, white, yellow, blue, gold and silver.

In terms of cultivation, this progression was usually accomplished in two stages, the first preliminary, and the second advanced. The preliminary stage keeps the attention split between the subjective or inner world and objective reality.

It utilizes the eyes Half-Open, Half-Closed Method as detailed earlier. Because of this split field, there becomes a more concrete linkage between the power of the light and the physical body. The second technique uses the eyes closed method. To briefly review.

1 - Shut your eyes.
2 - Place your inner visual attention in the center of your inner screen.
3 - Now move your focal point some distance 'away.'
4 - Lower your physical eyes as though falling asleep.
5 - While doing this, maintain the line of your inner visual focus at the distance you chose, rather than letting it change and follow the eyes downward as it normally would in the objective world.

Under normal circumstances, especially in a darkened room there will be some form of light. But be careful. If you look directly at it, it will seem to go away. The secret to success in this regard, is to use an *oblique* focus.

A variation of the split-field method is that instead of a top and bottom split, we move our conscious visual awareness away from our central focal point, a little to the right or left or above or below or a combination of both.

The idea is to hold our inner peripheral focus on our original line of sight or reference point, while shifting our main focus slightly off center.

When you become adept at doing this, you will find the light begins to grow, expand and intensify. When you can allow this to happen long enough, experiences may occur that are literally not of this world.

Knowing what lies beyond this world and beyond death has been mankind's wish for forever. If one is gifted with one of these experiences, the chances are they will no longer fear death.

# POSITIVE SENSATIONS - CONFIRMATORY SIGNS

One element that has been lacking in Zhan Zhuang literature is an inventory of specific confirmatory signs of correct practice. All that most people have heard of are the usual generalities like euphoria, a sense of power, emptiness, etc.

Of course these *are* real confirmatory signs and when a practitioner does experience one or more of them, they definitely know they're on the right track.

The trouble with the above mentioned sensations is that they can take years of dedicated practice, before being experienced. In the mean time, one often has the feeling much like wandering in the desert, in terms of if they're doing it right or not.

A *Yiquan* lineage teacher once told me, "You have to do it right. Some people practice for an hour and gain nothing!" So you can see the importance of some benchmarks, especially during the first years of training, in order to develop confidence and understanding.

The first and most simple sign is, to recognize that it's easier to go through your session than it was a month or three months earlier. This is so basic, it's easy to overlook. But really one has had to have achieved a greater degree of relaxation than they had when they started, in order to experience this.

So, now one can see the importance of cultivating awareness of the subtle. This is the essence of Zhan Zhuang and clearly relates to how Zhan Zhuang expands awareness. The idea is that through continued practice, we gradually develop greater perception on multiple levels.

There are confirmatory signs of correct practice for most degrees of achievement. For the new learner however, all but the most basic will be in that third circle of the diagram, 'beyond current perception.' But don't let that bother you, many of these signs will come with time. Meanwhile, we will focus on what most people *can* feel, that is the muscles.

In addition to the lengthening and/or widening discussed previously, there is a phenomenon that begins to occur when several adjoining muscles in a specific area have opened properly. There becomes a feeling that these individual muscles have linked or joined and become one. So we have the feeling of a relaxed unity, of no resistance. This feeling will expand over time to include more and more of the body, and is often felt most clearly at first, in the upper back and shoulder girdle area.

For example, the Trapezius opens and links to the Rhomboids which link with the shoulder blades and the Subscapularis muscle (on the inside of the shoulder blade) which in turn joins with the Teres muscles, the Deltoids, Triceps and Biceps, etc., all the way out to the finger tips.

The whole region then feels at ease, with no sense of resistance or effort in keeping the arms aloft. This leads to the notion of emptiness or sensing a non-physicality, or what might best be described as a Supra-Physical reality. This is in fact, an aspect of ourselves that is always present, and which we can tune into using Zhan Zhuang.

The thing about all of this is, no matter if you train every day with a great teacher, all he or she can do is point the way through example and explanation. Each and every learner must walk their own path alone. In other words, *it's up to each of us to make the system become a living reality inside ourselves*. Below is a list of positive physical and energetic signs that will let you know good things are happening and that you're doing something right.

**Relaxation**

The first sign is usually a feeling of greater relaxation. This leads to the second, a sense of ease while standing. This sense of ease generates a feeling of more space inside. This leads to a feeling of roundness like there's nothing angular in the body, no corners or sharp edges.

When I have observed some master Tai Chi practitioners train their form, their movements are so fluid, they appear to have no bones or joints. This speaks to the feeling of roundness we just mentioned. Also there is the state of calmness and tranquillity of the body, emotion and mind or a combination of all three.

**Warmth**

A feeling of warmth in the low Dan Tien or anywhere in the body is a sign that the Chi is moving and has become abundant enough to well up. This more localized warmth can then spread throughout the abdomen, torso and extremities and eventually the entire body. Where as, there are occasions when heat can indicate a blockage of some sort, the confirmatory sign of warmth, brings with it a sense of soothing or relaxation to the region where it is found.

**Lightness**

The arms feel very light as if they weigh little or nothing. It becomes effortless to hold up your arms, such that they almost seem to disappear. This form of lightness can also occur in the legs, but is often experienced *after* the stand through movement, meaning, during one's *Yiquan* or Tai Chi walking or the Tai Chi form for example.

**Heaviness**
The feet and/or legs feel like a clay or marble statue, cemented into the ground. This can also apply to the upper body as well. Another positive sign is the feeling of being sucked or pulled into the earth. There can also be a feeling of heaviness or solidity in the feet, while the rest of the body seems to weigh nothing. Please note: for the beginner, feelings of heaviness often indicate a blockage of some sort.

**Internal Movement**
We perceive some aspect of the inner workings of the body which was previously unavailable to our conscious awareness, like feeling the blood move. Or one can feel some energetic movement within the stillness of a posture. These movements can be energetically neutral or they can be charged with electricity, warmth, coolness or the sensation of wind or flowing water.

**Pulsing Sensations**
These are feelings of Chi energy pulsing through part or all of the body. This is mostly energetic, although there is an abstract physical feeling as well. This is different from the earlier description of internal movement, in that there is a definite pulsing or ebb and flow.

**Sense of Power**
When the previous physical feelings become amplified we can often feel a sudden sense of power or indomitability. This is especially true if our point of focus has been the low Dan Tien, the body's physical power center. This power can feel both martial and/or sexual. There is also a sense of invulnerability that can occur. Chi Kung masters who can have a car roll over their abdomen are in this state.

**Connection**
We feel a subtle but nevertheless concrete connection, linkage

or joining of our energy with the energy of the environment that surrounds us. The fact is, this connection already exists, for without it, we could not be alive here on Earth.

**Euphoria**

Often, after many of the previous sensations have been experienced, we may enter into a state of deep calmness or stillness. This can trigger various feelings of euphoria or ecstasy. These can stem from the Chi abundantly permeating the body or energizing centers in the brain. It may also be due to the influx of external energy entering, for example the entrance of Heaven or Earth Chi into the open conduit of the body, especially when the two meet and are in equal abundance.

**Hollowness**

When the organism has been flooded with large amounts of Chi, such that the flow permeates every atom of a particular location or the body as a whole, we may begin to feel a sense of hollowness, like there's an outer 'crust' of structure that is virtually empty inside. This can sometimes manifest as a feeling that all the soft tissue disappears and we are only aware of our bone structure.

**Emptiness**

When we have trained long enough and encountered many of the previous states of consciousness, we may find that the edges or outermost part of our body seem to disappear altogether, so that it is impossible to tell where our body ends and the air or external energy around us begins. This can lead to the sensation that the whole body disappears and there is emptiness both within and without. If we can dwell in this feeling long enough, we begin to feel entirely insubstantial. At that point, it is very possible to enter the Void and temporarily move beyond time and space altogether.

## MAINTAINING CONTROL VS. LETTING GO

Although I've discussed aspects of this subject previously, there are some other elements that bear looking at, insofar as they go to the core of Zhan Zhuang transformation.

Zhan Zhuang has two essential aspects to it. The first of these, maintaining control, stems from the Taoist Fire path. The other is letting go and trusting. This finds its origin in the Taoist Water method.

To understand the fire path, we look at the behavior of fire itself. Fire basically burns things up. And the hotter the fire gets, the more fuel it requires. Fire can also be erratic, witness a forest fire which starts in one location and then suddenly jumps to another. Or a fire can begin at one point, then fan out, igniting everything around it.

Water on the other hand, reacts somewhat more consistently. It can drip steadily so as to one day wear a hole through a rock. Or when more abundant, it can flow steadily like a river, or race and tumble like a set of rapids. Water can also be like the sea and ebb and flow or well up into an enormous wave.

These images and the one's above, can be interpreted as symbolic representations of both the movements of Chi, as well as the distinctions in developmental modus operandi. As a general rule, the fire method is usually more appropriate when one is younger, whereas the Water method is more suitable for those getting on in years.

The truth is, and this goes to the heart of the matter, we must learn to become comfortable with both. That is, letting go and to a certain extent, maintaining control. In the beginning, people often spend too much time trying to *rigidly* maintain postural control.

Of course this has its place. But it also has its drawbacks. It creates worry and an actual increase in tension that manifests in many practitioners. This can lead to the development of *Yang* strength, but not the deeper, more mysterious *Yin* strength. To cultivate *Yin* power, we must let go of how we think and feel about how we make power. And that means consciously letting go of the *Yang* Frame we have been so diligently cultivating.

We must trust. Trust that all the work we've done has been incorporated into the subconscious and will manifest as a proper conduit no matter what our posture.

As one's *Yin* power grows, the exterior look of their posture becomes less and less important, because through decades of due diligence the conduit of the body is open.

So, the idea is to set up your posture as best you can, then turn to letting go as much as possible within the structure. This includes allowing the body to slightly modify your position to achieve a greater amount of relaxation.

The body will always take the line of least resistance. This means that it will seek to micro-adjust and modify one's posture in an effort to find a greater and greater sense of Central Equilibrium, meaning a greater sense of ease, relaxation, well-being and balance.

This speaks to another important point, surrendering to the body's innate wisdom. The body will, of itself, correct many imbalances if we're willing to stand back, get out of our own way and *let it*. This *is Wu Wei*. Remember, the idea of this letting go in order to cultivate power, is a primary difference between the Zhan Zhuang approach and the hard martial art styles, including many *Kung Fu* schools.

# ADDITIONAL TECHNIQUES

## THE POUNDING EXERCISE

The Pounding Exercise uses the back of loosely held fists to tap or hit down the *Huato Jiaji* and Bladder meridians of the back. It is best done as a two-person exercise, but can also be done, if only in part, as a solo practice, still to great benefit.

Begin by facing your training partner's back and locating their *Dazhui* point, just above the Big Vertebra, at the base of the neck.

Place the soft part of each fist on either side of it. It is important to note here that under no circumstances at any time during the exercise, should you make contact with the bones of the spine.

The *Huato Jiaji* meridian is what we're looking for. It's located just to the outside of the Spinous Processes of the vertebrae. This is generally 1/3 to 1/2 an inch to the outside of where you can feel bone.

The actual action of pounding requires rapid back-and-forth alternation of loosely formed fists, which then begin to move slowly all the way down the back and then down onto the Sacrum itself.

There are several descending depressions in the Sacrum called Sacral Foramen, which when stimulated, have a great ability to release tension in the lower back and hips. The prohibition against hitting spinal vertebrae does not apply to the Sacrum or hip bones.

In order to reach the speed required to make the exercise effective, one must retain loose, relaxed wrists and by no means hit too hard. It's best to start with a light rapid tapping strength which does not penetrate too deeply into the body. The best way is to ask the person being pounded to set the strength of the hitting. As with most things of this nature, the

Rule of the Golden Mean applies. "Don't do too much and don't do too little." In other words not too light and not too hard.

Now, the idea with the hitting is to create an even back and forth rhythm, much like playing the conga drums. This even, non-stop repetitive rhythm is needed to trigger the necessary response from the 'poundee's' brain.

The idea with this is, by setting up a fast repetitive rhythm of the right intensity, we use the nerves, to in a sense, trick the brain. It goes something like this. Each time we make impact with a fist, the nerves send a message to the brain. The rapid repetition therefore generates many, many messages or impulses. Because they're coming so fast, the brain has trouble coping and finally sends a general signal to the region being stimulated, to just *let go*.

And it works. After one has pounded down the three meridian lines of the exercise, the partner will feel a definite and sometimes profound release of tension and hence, far greater relaxation overall.

Now for the other two meridian lines, in this case both are Bladder meridians. Bladder line 1 is found about two inches or so, lateral to the centerline of the spine. The points on this line are called *Shu* or father points and are significant, in that by pounding them, we access and stimulate every organ in the body. The nerves along this line of the back enervate their respective organs directly.

So, you follow the same procedure as before. Find the partner's Big Vertebra then place the fists two to three inches on either side of it and repeat the same procedure as with the *Jiaji* line. Be sure to include the Sacrum which, as long as a person hasn't been injured there, can take an increased degree of impact to great effect. There are more *Shu* points on the Sacrum, Small Intestine and Bladder for example, so don't forget to properly follow through, all the way down.

Now we come to the third meridian, which we'll call the Bladder 2 line and the conclusion of the exercise. The Bladder 2 line is found differently from the first two. This line is found just to the inside of the shoulder blade. Use the point on the Scapula closest to the centerline of the body as your guideline.

Start up near the top of the shoulders and begin pounding down as before until you reach the lowest rib. This is the line of demarcation. Below this, until you reach the hipbone, you must now greatly reduce the strength of your hitting to avoid injuring the Kidneys which lie directly beneath. Once you feel bone again (the hip bone) you can finish with an even stronger than normal force if you like. The Bladder 2 line should finish in the buttocks region lateral (to the outside) of the Sacrum bone.

There is one last factor regarding the Bladder 2 line and it is quite interesting. Along the Bladder 2 line, situated level with where the Shu points enervate the organs, are five locations of note. These are the access points of the psychic elements of the five Yin Organs. They are:

| Organ | Acupuncture Point | Psychic Component |
|---|---|---|
| Lungs | Pohu BL-42 | *Po* - Corporeal Soul |
| Heart | Shentang Bl-44 | *Shen* - Spirit Emperor |
| Liver | Hunmen Bl-47 | *Hun* - Etheric Soul |
| Spleen | Yishe BL-49 | *Yi* - Intellect |
| Kidneys | Zhishi Bl-52 | *Zhi* - the Will |

Stimulating any of these points can generate or release emotional content stored in the body's cellular memory.

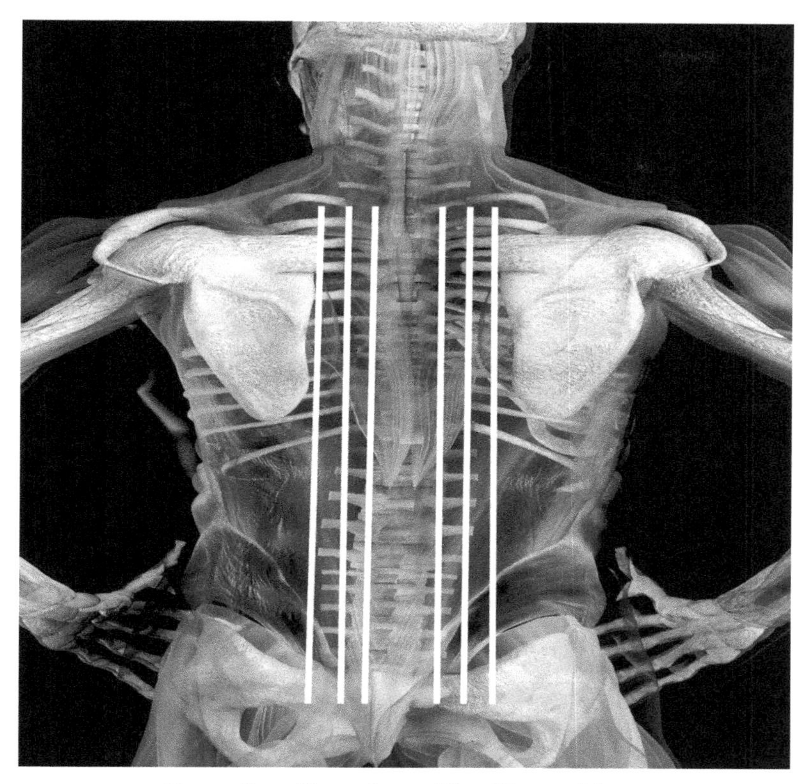

**Pounding Exercise - The Three Lines**

## AROUND THE WORLD MEDITATION

This method circulates the Chi through all the acupuncture meridians at the level of the *Wei Chi* and *Ying Chi*. *Wei Chi* is the body's external defensive or immune system energy and *Ying Chi* is the body's Nutritive Chi, which travels with the blood.

The technique utilizes Chinese Medicine's times of organ circulation for it's order of progression. These are the two hour periods throughout each 24 hour cycle.

Following this model, the meridian order for this exercise is: Lungs, Large Intestine, Stomach, Spleen, Heart, Small Intestine, Bladder, Kidneys, Pericardium, Triple Burner, Gall Bladder, Liver.

Naturally, this is an advanced technique, but that said, it is not necessary to know the location of every acupuncture point along the various pathways. However, to employ this method, there are several things which must be learned. Acquiring, or at least having online access to diagrams for each meridian individually, as well as on the body as a whole, is strongly advised.

To begin with, one finds the location of the origin and end points for each meridian. Notice that the end point of one meridian is in the same relative region as the origin point of the next.

Finding these locations visually and knowing where they are mentally is absolutely necessary, but ultimately it is the ability to feel these locations throughout the body that becomes paramount.

A good way to acquire this feeling-awareness is to simply press an origin point firmly and hold that pressure for a few moments. When you stop, you should still be able to feel the location. From there, proceed to tracing along the line of the meridian with your finger to acquire a feeling-sense of it, in it's entirety. Later, you will use this awareness to move the Chi through all the meridians.

**List of Channel Origin and End Points**

| CHANNEL | ORIGIN POINT | END POINT |
|---|---|---|
| LUNG | LU-1 Zhongfu | LU-11 Shaoshang |
| LARGE INTESTINE | LI-1 Shangyang | LI-20 Yingxiang |
| STOMACH | ST-1 Chengqi | ST-45 Lidui |
| SPLEEN | SP-1 Yinbai | SP-21 Dabao |
| HEART | HT-1 Jiquan | HT-9 Shaochong |
| SMALL INTESTINE | SI-1 Shaoze | SI-19 Tinggong |
| BLADDER | BL-1 Jingming | BL-67 Zhiyin |
| KIDNEYS | K-1 Yongquan | K-27 Shufu |
| PERICARDIUM | P-1 Tianchi | P-9 Zhongchong |
| TRIPLE BURNER | TB-1 Guanchong | TB-23 Sizhukong |

| GALL BLADDER | GB-1 Tongziliao | GB-44 Qiaoyin |
|---|---|---|
| LIVER | LIV-1 Dadun | LIV-14 Qimen |
| GOVERNING VESSEL | GV-1 Changqiang | GV-28 Yinjiao |
| CONCEPTION VESSEL | CV-1 Huiyin | CV-24 Chengjiang |

The idea behind this method is to 'feel' your way along the pathways and in so doing move the Chi. With the longer meridians, this can be done first in sections. What you're trying to do, is to be able to feel your way along the channels *as if* feeling your finger were lightly tracing the route.

This is a preliminary step which will get you through until such time as your Chi is abundant enough, and your *Nei Kung* control complete enough, so that you can put your attention in a Channel origin point and then, by simply moving or jumping your feeling-awareness to the next major point on the route, you feel as though a sensation of warmth or lukewarm water flowed along the pathway in between.

When you have completed the cycle of the twelve organs, it's best to end by circulating the Chi several times through the Microcosmic Orbit. Go up the *Du* meridian or Governing Vessel in back then *down* the *Ren* Meridian or Conception Vessel in front, passing through the low Dan Tien each time. Finally, on the last repetition, lead the Chi down the *Ren* Meridian and into the low Dan Tien.

Around The World Meditation is a powerful and effective technique and if practiced daily, will greatly improve the health of the body.

## STANDING'S LINK WITH TAI CHI

A secret hides in plain sight. What secret? That Zhan Zhuang's most basic stance, the Wuji posture, is embedded in all Tai Chi styles.

The answer lies in the very beginning of the Tai Chi form, just prior to Commencement. What are we doing then? Probably standing with our feet parallel, somewhere between shoulder and hip width, depending on style. And there it is, one of the biggest secrets of Tai Chi, hiding in plain sight.

The truth is, the original Tai Chi lineage practice contained Zhan Zhuang training. The practitioners of old often stood in the Wuji posture, arms resting at their sides, just as they are prior to Commencement, for an hour or more before beginning their form repetitions.

So, for the serious practitioner, it is important to incorporate Zhan Zhuang as a fundamental part of the Tai Chi curriculum. This becomes apparent when we examine the example of *Yang Cheng Fu*.

*Yang* was taught Zhan Zhuang by his father and uncle, but only showed it to a handful of people. Why? Because Zhan Zhuang generates, activates and enhances the 'engine' that effectively drives the Chi flow during Tai Chi practice.

In other words, when *Yang* showed someone standing meditation, he knew they could potentially develop genuine internal power. No wonder he was so reticent in imparting it.

My own experience in this regard may shed some more light. When I was just starting out, I found a knowledgeable teacher and after he saw me execute the form, he said something like, "Oh, you have the external, now all I have to do is teach you Tai Chi."

This felt a little insulting at the time, what with my solid martial arts background and all, but I would come to know the truth of what he had proclaimed.

What the Sifu was saying, was that my form looked okay on the outside, but there was nothing going on, on the inside, under the skin. It took me many years to subconsciously internalize all the various elements. But it wasn't until Zhan Zhuang came into the mix, that the sayings in the Tai Chi Classics began to manifest.

The body is like a car and the Chi is the fuel. The trouble with most people at the beginning, is that their car only has a frame and outer body, but lacks a good engine. By engine, I mean the mechanism that most efficiently and abundantly transports the Chi, in order to facilitate the smooth running of all the body's physical and energetic systems.

In terms of linkage, Zhan Zhuang is the *Yin* to Tai Chi's *Yang*. In Zhan Zhuang we stand still and things move inside. In Tai Chi we aim for stillness while in movement. Together, the two create the complete package, both for health as well as for internal martial power.

A perfect example of this is when you see master practitioners doing Push Hands with real internal power and very little or no movement. There are a number of videos on YouTube, the one's with *Ma Yue Liang* come to mind. Anyway, when you see what they can do, you can know pretty much without a doubt, that each has passed through the gate of Zhan Zhuang and has incorporated the enhanced awareness and power into their Tai Chi and Push Hands movements.

## ZHAN ZHUANG AND FA JING

Fa Jing is a vast subject in and of itself. The explanation of the details of the numerous types of Fa Jing available to the advanced practitioner would fill several volumes. That said, there are a number of common factors necessary for any form of Fa Jing to manifest and it is here where Zhan Zhuang can fulfill a critical role.

Before any form of proper Fa Jing can be manifested, the body will of had to have reached a good degree of integration and unification, which is just what occurs when exercising with standing meditation. In addition to this, one will have achieved 'spring power' and the ability to make their energy-body spherical.

By 'spring power,' I am referring to the unification of the various muscles groups and sinews (springs) into one whole-body, integrated spring. This whole body spring power is the physical basis upon which the more internal, spherical types of Fa Jing are based.

There are three general components associated with Spherical Fa Jing. A horizontal component, a vertical component and a radial or depth component. The horizontal component manifests as a lateral movement, the rapid closing (folding) and opening (unfolding) of the Kua. This can most easily be executed in the sequence, *Open, Close, Open*. But the key is the rhythm with which they are implemented.

We will turn to music for a further explanation and use the eighth note and quarter note relationship. This relationship can be expressed metronomically as 2:1 or two to one, that is, in the rhythmic space of one quarter note there can be two eighth notes. So the rhythm of the horizontal delivery would be *Open -- Close-Open*. In other words, the closing and second kua opening at the moment of release, happen twice as fast as the first opening. You would count, 1 -- 2,3. This rhythmic component gathers and then amplifies the Chi before issuing.

The second or vertical component is the ability to condense and lengthen the body from the top of the head to the bottoms of the feet. Simply put, it is becoming shorter and taller. But the key is of course, how we do it. For Spherical Fa Jing, we condense from the top of the head down, into the centerpoint and from the bottoms of the feet up to the centerpoint.

This is usually done first in simple, linear-like vertical motions, but later, this becomes a spiral mechanism. Spiraling inward from the extremities to our centerpoint while closing and condensing, then spiraling outward from our centerpoint back out to the extremities, feet and hands while opening and expanding.

Lastly there is the depth component. This can be thought of as the ability to expand backward and forward at the same time. This movement creates the third plane (along with horizontal and vertical) and hence the three-dimensionality of the sphere. This depth plane of movement is further enhanced and reinforced by the tailbone movement of releasing downward *then* tucking under.

On a physical level, Fa Jing is based on the 'springs' of the body and the ability to instantly load and unload these springs with a greater and greater amount of 'weight' or torque force. The more springs we have working in unified-coordination, the greater the amount of compression and therefore the greater release of spring power.

Again on a physical level, in the beginning these springs are our muscles, tendons and ligaments, combined with a certain form of spinal compression. In the progression of learning, we must first master the correct outer form using larger motions, then smaller motions and finally very little or even no *apparent* motion. Therefore we would do well to train and condition the body with the more visible *Yang Chi* energies first. This creates a unified vessel, through which later, the less visible *Yin Chi* forms of Fa Jing will flow and be issued. This vessel or conduit can be thought of as one's 'frame.'

The idea behind the method is much like a musician practicing scales, or Tai Chi's use of slow practice. In other words, meticulous and methodical.

At first, we use an exaggerated sense of condensing (loading the springs) and expanding. (releasing the springs) This is what's known as bigger motion. Then, once everything is working in the large frame, we reduce the overall size of the movements needed to medium size, and then later to small frame that looks almost like a shiver.

This means that we can issue the same amount of power we derived from the large frame/big motion, using a smaller and smaller space within which the movements happen. The idea is to reduce the size of the big motions to a tiny space, but still with all the components functioning as with the large frame. What takes us let's say, one foot distance to discharge in large frame takes only 6 inches in medium frame and 1 to 2 inches or less in small frame. In other words making the movement more and more internal or 'under the skin,' so to speak.

The reason for this is obvious. In life or death combat, all we have (besides technique) are what we feel and what we see. If our movements are exceedingly small and extremely fast, the less time the opponent will have to recognize and react. The Classics say, "...I know the opponent but the opponent does not know me."

So, how do we make all this happen? The idea is to discover and develop what we'll call Spherical Movement. "When one part moves, all parts move." As stated earlier, at the beginning it is necessary to develop all the appropriate linkages to our centerpoint/low Dan Tien.

Once these have been achieved, it's time to put it all to work. The idea is the ability to create a very small sphere during closing and then expand it at the speed of thought to a large sphere, either physically or energetically or both.

This is a basic generic method. After it is mastered, there are many more details that must be learned in order to apply it to the large variety of specific issuing methods, such as working with the flow of certain Channels, bringing Chi from the bones to the surface, using organ energy, combining Heaven and Earth energies and more.

Let's first examine the physics of what happens when a large sphere condenses to a small sphere. The shrinkage takes place equally from all directions. In terms of the body, we can think of this as vertical, horizontal and radial movement to and from our centerpoint. This is the basic Tai Chi Fa Jing method. Note: *Everything I am about to describe will inevitably have to be done simultaneously to produce the desired result and is best learned one on one from a discerning Sifu.*

**Lower Body Condensing**

Now, in order to reduce the sphere, imagine you're in a Bow Stance. First, condense the tissue from below the feet, up into your centerpoint. In the large frame, this means the distance between our feet and navel is visibly reduced.

At the same time as the vertical distance is being reduced, the length of the posture must be energetically 'squeezed' shorter as well, in other words, the distance between the front and back foot. And finally, the distance between the outsides of the feet, legs, hips and kua must also be condensed into the centerpoint. If you have properly hardwired stretching and especially spiraling the tissue, this should occur relatively automatically.

**Upper Body Condensing**

For the upper body, visualize your arms in the *An* or Push posture. We start by condensing the distance between the top of the head and navel area. *This includes all the tissue from the fingers through the shoulders into the body's centerline*. Now, just like with the lower body, while condensing vertically from the head to the navel, also condense the distance between front and back and between your left and right sides.

Note: The longer the stance horizontally, the less vertical movement is possible. The shorter the stance, the more vertical movement is possible, while horizontal movement is restricted. This does not include rotation energy, which is in fact enhanced. This is one of the reasons why the small frame, short stances offer so much flexibility.

Now it's time to put it all together. That was the first half, condensing the sphere. Now in order to issue, everything is applied in reverse. Energetic movement initiates from the centerpoint and after much practice, expands in all directions simultaneously. For this to happen, we must hardwire the directional expansion of the movement in a sequence that will later be performed in unison. Again imagine yourself in the *An* posture.

Assuming you've condensed properly, first expand from your centerpoint downward into your feet, *especially* into your back foot. At the same time, expand the distance between the centerpoint and the outside of your back and the outside of your chest and abdomen.

This expansion should percolate outwards and inflate the arms. As it does, simultaneously expand the distance between the centerpoint and *Baihui* at the top of the head, while also expanding the distances between the centerpoint and each side.

The idea behind this sequence comes from the Classics, "...if there's a top, there's a bottom, if there's a left, there's a right..." "If you want to go up, first go down, if you want to go right, first go left..." So now we can see that the basic understanding of how to issue Fa Jing has been stated in the Classics all along.

**Reducing and Expanding the Sphere**

To summarize, while condensing the lower half of the body upward and inward toward our centerpoint, we simultaneously condense the upper half of the body downward and inward into the same location.

Now, in order to issue power, we expand everything from our center out to all our extremities. Downward and backward, forward and upward. Take the Yang Tai Chi Brush Knee posture for example.

If we want the power to come out our forward palm, it is important that we send energy to our back, the back leg and the palm-down hand at our hip, rather than focusing solely on the hand through which the actual discharge will be issued.

We haven't spoken of breath here yet, but suffice it to say, one can use either normal breath (inhale, expand, exhale, condense) or reverse breath, which more closely parallels the actual directions of the sphere's expansion and contraction. (inhale, abdomen withdraws, exhale, abdomen expands) The speed at which one practices is also worth some attention. The odd thing about Fa Jing is that it is easier learn when *not* done too slowly. You've already put in plenty of slow practice in the hardwiring stages. So, one starts by using a moderate speed, not too fast at the beginning. Only after this is hardwired, do you progress to faster speeds. All this refers to the large frame movement.

Once we can execute the larger movement properly, pretty much at full speed, then it's time to reduce the size of the stance and distance of the movement. From large to medium and finally to small, all the while retaining the original power or in fact, actually increasing it. Once we can achieve power with little or no distance, with enough one-pointed standing meditation, it becomes possible to almost eliminate movement in favor of pure *Yi* which leads the Chi, which moves the blood.

Once the basic methods have been internalized, a number of higher level practices become possible, like the ability to shift one's center and issue power from any point in the body or the use of vibrational energy to disrupt body functions or break bones.

Energetically there are even more techniques including how to shape the Chi as you discharge, that is, making it sharper or more diffuse or using the *Kan - Li* , water and fire relationship, or even the Heaven and Earth energies themselves. These last two techniques often generate a bio-electromagnetic shock (like an electric shock) as part of the discharge. It is said that the great Chen style Master of the last century, *Chen Fa Ke* manifested such a feeling when he discharged his disciples.

Here are links to two of my videos on YouTube which illustrate much of what has been described here.
http://www.youtube.com/watch?v=HW4krTtrOv8
http://www.youtube.com/watch?v=FNBhhC5_634

# EPILOGUE

It is my sincere wish that the material presented in this book will have added to your storehouse of knowledge. You are now aware of some new and exciting possibilities that can be incorporated into your practice. Those who are willing to explore these techniques and train faithfully will find their achievement growing by leaps and bounds. This means an improvement in both one's health and martial power.

For those who don't have a knowledgeable teacher readily available, it is hoped that this work will also serve as an insightful reference and perhaps even an inspiration.

The possibilities for growth are nearly unlimited. As we augment our Kung Fu through daily Zhan Zhuang practice, these newly acquired achievements will also show up as an enhanced quality in our everyday lives.

*Zhu Ni Chenggong*

Aloha,
Mark Cohen

# ADDITIONAL PLATES

# ADDITIONAL PLATES

Parallel Stance - Hip Width

Shoulder Width

Narrow Width

**Wuji Posture - Natural Position - Side View**

**Taoist Position - Side View**

**Shoulder-Stretch Position - Side View**

**Beaks Position - Side View**

Closed-Fist Position - Side View

Internal Organ Postures - Kidneys - Side View

**Author in a Bagua Cultivation Posture**

## ABOUT THE AUTHOR

Mark Cohen has lineage in Yiquan and the Yang and Wu Styles of Tai Chi Chuan. He also holds belts in Shotokan Karate and Hwa Rang Do and a seventh generation lineage in Chinese Medicine.

Contact:
9heavenchigung@hawaii.rr.com

# INDEX

## F



## G



## H



## I

## *T*

## U



## V



## W



## X



## Y

*ACKNOWLEDGMENTS*

*Mahalo Nui Loa*

*Michael*

*Stuart*

*Cynthia*

*Archie*

*Without your benevolence*
*this book would not have been possible.*

*And on a special note, I would particularly like to express my gratitude to Sifu Fong Ha for sharing the essence of Yiquan and for his generosity and inspiration these past 27 years.*

CPSIA information can be obtained
at www.ICGtesting.com
Printed in the USA
LVHW051104240119
605081LV00007B/38/P